OUT OF MY SCULL

Mayhem & Misadventures on Delaware's Christina River

DANIELLE J BATTAGLIA

OUT OF MY SCULL
THE WACKY WORLD OF RECREATIONAL ROWING

© 2024, Danielle J Battaglia.

Copyright registration number TXu 2-420-757.
Effective date of registration: March 13, 2024.
Registration decision date: March 28, 2024

Print ISBN: 979-8-35095-171-4
eBook ISBN: 979-8-35096-768-5

For Ann, Linda and Lou

Contents

Preface

Most of you are familiar with competitive rowing. Dan Brown brought to the world's attention the stunning tale of a University of Washington sweep crew and their unlikely path to rowing victory in the 1936 Olympics. This is a fantastic tale of perseverance, strength, diligence, dedication, and longing for success. Stories like this one warm our souls, inspire our imaginations, and spark our own longings to be the best,

But rowing has a sleepy side called recreational. Adult crews row for fun and enjoy the same benefits of camaraderie, teamwork, and friendship without the pressure of serious competition. After a row at the local bar or coffee shop, we can be found performing the familiar "atta girls" for our crew while unapologetically criticizing another crew's pitiful performance. Crews didn't invent this behavior. It has been practiced by non-pro teams of basketball, football, and baseball since the Mayans.

Rec crews must recognize the value of good technique and continual improvement. These are at the top of all rowers' agendas because rows are difficult and frustrating without decent technique. Enthusiasts who insist on marching to their own tune in a boat that requires balance and synchronization soon become pariahs—the pitiful ones left shuffling their feet after all crews choose their team members. It only takes one of these folks to cock up a row for everyone. Rec rowers choose not to compete regularly. They form primarily by luck, sometimes just by who stands next to whom at the boathouse. They survive together by conforming to each other's style.

Out of My Scull is the story of my tap dance through myriad (mis)adventures, mishaps, and mayhem, some of which have taken my breath away. There are a few peculiar if not downright outrageous characters (a couple of them husbands) who bring their tango to the party, and a smattering of uncanny nonhuman species adding some spicy salsa. Ultimately, this dance dumps me onto the sliding seat of a scull. From this exalted position, I marvel at the absurdity of rowing, showing you the sport's fun and funny side and the amazing opportunity to develop friendships.

Picture driving backward on anything—a bike, a car, a little red wagon—using some dime-store spy glasses or a dental mirror dangling from your visor to enlighten you about where you are headed, or trusting your life to an elf-sized coxswain who is the only one who is facing where you are going and not contributing a lick of power to the effort.

And for this dicey experience, your crew must lift and carry a two-hundred-pound boat to the water from its storage perch. Inevitably, someone on your crew pretends to carry their share of the weight, substantially increasing your burden. Once on the water, your crew must balance in a boat with a rounded bottom and no keel, and without rapt attention, they will roll over and dump everyone into the river. All of this amidst specially coined words and phrases like "waynuf," catch a crab," "skying," "hold water," and the most common, "oh shit."

The same enthusiasm, joy, and warm fuzzies experienced at an arena full of fans enjoying a concert, football game, or anything is also part of the rowing experience. These feelings occur because a gathering of humanoids doing the same thing at the same time releases endorphins and fosters goodwill and trust among them. Add to that the spell of the natural world in which we row—on the river, watching each season glow and fade, sharing space with other living critters going about their daily tasks—and you have nirvana.

Those who row recreationally get all these benefits without losing their summer weekends to regattas and living with continual anxiety of winning the next big race. You take your life into your hands, sign a waiver promising you will not hold your boat club responsible for any loss of limbs, brain damage, or otherwise dire bodily damage, and jump in. What's not to love? Well, if you continue to read, all will be revealed.

This nonfiction story is based on reality, but I have used some creative license. Not all tales are described exactly as they happened or involve the people I've placed in the scenes. The characters are drawn as I see them, not necessarily as they are. I apologize to those rowers who think they find themselves among these pages if my characterization offends you. It's all meant to be in good fun.

CHAPTER 1

Oh, What a Beautiful Morning

Freed at last from the world's chaotic madness and the minutia muddying up our own little lives, we were lulled by the rhythm, soothed by the calm water, and hushed by the sun's warmth on our skin. The air was cool, the birds were singing, the fish were jumping, and the geese were paddling. There was nothing but peace in our corner of the universe until the wicked river gremlins showed up and created an event having the same effect on us as if we had mainlined three espressos.

"Port oars out, one foot in, and down,"

"Count down when ready. Bow."

"Two."

"Three."

"Four."

"Hands on the dock and big shove."

We hang onto our oars and push the scull away from the dock. We commence our warm-up. "Sit at the finish and row."

Our eighteen-inch wide, forty-five-foot long scull skims quietly through the still waters, barely creating a ripple. We are enthralled by the trees in spring's early bud lining the river, supporting the cloudless powder-blue sky, reflected on the water's smooth surface and creating a second wavy version of this lovely morning.

Sitting in a single file, we move as vertebrae, separate but tethered. At the beginning of our stroke, we bend our knees to our chests and stretch our arms forward and outward to the limit our bodies will allow. At that peak, we simultaneously drop oars into the water, thrust hard with our legs, pivot at our hips, and change body direction quickly as a swimmer at the turn of a lap. We gracefully glide forward to find that perfect stroke position again while watching our blades pepper the smooth surface with tiny droplets, creating mini-eddies.

A riffle of water rushes along the stern as the bow diverts the river, slicing through its mirrored surface. The loudest sound is a steady, rhythmic clunk of oars in the oarlocks as blades feather, enter, and exit the river in unison. Our scull is a tropical fish glittering on the water, offering its pointed, sleek fore and aft decks to the shimmering morning ballet.

We turn upriver today, away from the city's noise, steel, and concrete. Away from the kids on the shore singing "row, row, row your boat." Away from the fishermen who don't even look up, so intent are they on their lines; away from couples who don't notice us as they walk the boardwalk hand in hand. And away from others who stop, rest their arms over the railing at the water's edge, and quietly watch our passing while their dogs sit patiently by their side, waiting for the morning walk to resume.

Upriver is a quieter scene, without humans singing, waving, or ignoring us, especially in the early morning. Seagulls and cormorants line the piers, looking to snag their day's first meal. Turtles, large and small, are crawling out of the water onto logs at sloth pace, craning their heads side to side in search of a sun puddle to warm their reptilian bodies from the night's coolness.

River snakes slither gracefully through the water, only their heads venturing above the smooth surface, anxious to hide in the tall reeds at the bank as daylight continues to reveal itself. Muskrats and gophers are thrashing their way out of the safety of the rushes to find the river's edge and a cool morning drink.

Geese honk overhead, and we are blessed with a white egret resplendent on her elegant long legs, drying her magnificent, vast wingspan amid the reeds. Momma ducks are leading the newborn ducklings on their exciting first water outings. Osprey's mom and dad are tirelessly feeding their hatchling's demanding cries. An eagle interrupts her search for breakfast to watch us move through her territory. A doe wanders to the water to quench her thirst. Morning is a busy time for wildlife. But their busyness unfolds quietly. And our row is peaceful.

Here, our passing goes unacknowledged, although not unnoticed. Here, we get to be part of the morning's incredible unfolding, sensual, delicious magic. Here, we . . .

CRACK. "Uh oh."

CHAPTER 2

Damsels in Distress

The Christina River in Wilmington, Delaware, can beckon to you on a bright sunny day, but no one swims in it, even on the hottest summer day. It's a contaminated river, frequently the subject of potential reclamation projects upon which city officials run political campaigns but never quite put into place after the election.

It connects to a smaller river running through town into which the city sewage system flows when storm drains overflow. In the spring, with heavy rains, it is tough to avoid conjecturing what the baby-shit-brown–colored sludge floating on the surface might be. I'm told that chemicals were freely dumped into that river by local companies back then, so years of effluence have been added to the sewer soup.

Many years ago, a friend told me of an incident when she presented to her physician with a nasty wart on her finger. He said to her that she had three options: he could burn it off, cut it out, or she could dip it into the Christina River and wait a week for it to fall off. She chose the latter course and was delighted not to pay a doctor's bill.

And here we four are, in shock to find ourselves suddenly bobbing and blubbering in its nasty water on what began as a fine spring morning row.

"Is everyone okay?" Lou sputters.

"Yeah, I guess," Linda says from the other side of the overturned boat.

"Yeah, I'm okay," says Ann. "What happened?"

"Hit something, or something hit us. Anyone see anything?" I ask.

We four are the Panthers, a woman's recreational quad crew of good rowers who have been rowing together for years. We are an unlikely crew because of physical size differences, but we row well together and don't usually face anything similar to the current devastating predicament. We know that the river offers up debris with the changing tides, which can be substantial. That's why we are careful to watch where we are rowing.

"Can't see anything, but my feet are sinking into the damn mud on the bottom of this disgusting river," says Linda.

Linda is every inch Italian; her homemade limoncello is a favorite around the boathouse on barbeque nights. She's built for power, all muscle. Like most Italian mammas, she'd give anyone the shirt off her back. She's a natural take-charge person, always volunteering to deliver a homemade dinner to anyone temporarily incapacitated. She knows everyone, knows all the latest gossip, and can find humor in the smallest of life's happenings. She's protective of her brood, which includes her two daughters and rowing buddies.

From Lou, a nervous laugh, "I can't touch the bottom."

Lou is a tiny five feet and one hundred pounds, married with a daughter. She always has a smile on her face and kind words for everyone. Just below the smile, Lou has a perpetual laugh. Everything in her world is funny, making her great fun. She and Linda can get our quad laughing at pretty much nothing. And somehow, all that nothing is always hysterical.

"Maybe we can get the boat turned over and back in."

"Uh, not without riggers." At this point, we all notice that they have been sheared clean off.

"Oh my god!"

There is no way to row a boat with oars on just one side. We are doomed and dreading the need to be rescued, which is every rower's nightmare.

"Anyone got their cell phone?"

Linda pipes in, "I have mine. I'll call the boathouse."

The boat is now upside down with four of our eight oars still attached in oarlocks and riggers. But four other oars, attached to their oarlocks and riggers, are floating merrily about us.

"Can someone please grab the riggers and oars floating on that side," Lou, ever polite, asks.

"I've got these two," I say.

I'm Danielle, the boat's stroke seat. I'm fifty-eight, five feet four inches tall, and 130 pounds. I'm strong, but years of smoking destroyed my lungs, so I have significantly diminished my aerobic ability. I'm married, have no kids, and foolishly confident enough to try anything once.

"I've got the other two," grunts Ann as she reaches for the last oar and rigger. Ann is our other powerhouse. The tallest of the group at around five feet nine inches, she has a son and daughter just out of the house and is no longer married. She is the most experienced rower among the four of us, having taken rowing vacations with her kids when they were in high school.

While Linda calls the boathouse to rescue us, the rest of us stand sinking into the mud or, in Lou's case, treading water, trying to keep the boat and its broken pieces from drifting downriver with the tide. Oh, did I not mention that our river is tidal? One of its many challenges is a rather hefty tide that will carry sculls toward the myriad debris floating or stuck firmly in the mud, creating collision hazards for unsuspecting rowers. This morning, it is trying to drag the boat and us upriver away from our boathouse and into the considerably more significant, container-boat-trafficked Delaware River port.

"Yeah, the boat is upside down, we are in the water, and the starboard riggers are sheared off. We can't row it even if we could get in it. Can someone come and get us? We want to get out of this awful river before we are knee-deep in sludge. Thank you," says Linda.

"Who was there?" asks Lou, still wearing her black Roy Orbison–style spy sunglasses. The sunglasses are mirrored at the edges so bows can see behind them without turning around.

"Peter Myers. At least he knows how to drive a launch," says Linda.

"Oh, that's good," says Ann. "We have an experienced knight coming to our rescue." Still a little shell-shocked, we don't find this at all funny.

"I don't like being out here," says Lou, tired from treading water because she can't touch the bottom.

"That's an understatement."

"Lou, hang onto the boat, I say. We should all hang onto the boat. There is no need to touch the bottom and lose a sock." All rowers wear socks inside the boat shoes out of fear of catching athlete's foot, warts, or some other contagious, unheard-of, and incurable foot disease from others who row in the same shoes.

"Already lost mine," laughs Linda.

"I'm coming around to that side of the boat. I don't like being on this side alone," says Ann. "I'm alone enough as it is."

"Do you think we are drifting downstream?" asks Lou in a tiny voice.

"Ah, yeah, we probably are. The tide was going out," I say.

"Here, Ann, I can hold onto one of those oars while you come around. Just don't let go of the boat, okay?" says Linda.

"I'm fine," says Ann. "Uh-oh."

"What, what is it?" I ask.

"I lost hold of the other rigger. It's drifting toward your end, Lou," says Ann.

"Okay, okay, let me see if I can grab it. Hold on. Don't worry. I'll go around the end and . . ." says Lou.

"Don't let go of the boat!" shouts Linda in a panic. "Lou, Lou, say something. We can't see you. Are you okay?"

"Yeah, I'm okay. Got it," Lou shouts.

"Thank god," says Linda.

"Ann, you okay?" I ask.

"Yeah, did Lou get the rigger?"

"Yes. She's got it, and she's okay. Lou, you coming back around?"

"Thank god. The Board would probably have made me pay for that," says Ann, who is on the rowing club's Board.

"Yeah, I'm here." Lou materializes from the stern of the boat with a rigger part in one hand and a smile on her face. "One rescued rigger coming up."

"What a mess," declares Linda. "What the heck could we have hit?"

"I'm sorry, guys. I didn't see anything, and I was looking, believe me. Whatever it was, it must have been submerged. This is all my fault," declares Lou, accepting all the blame we are not putting on her shoulders.

"Oh, Lou, it's not your fault. We can't even see what we hit knowing something's there," says Linda.

"Maybe it was the river monster arising from the muddy depths to lure rowers into the murky waters," I say, trying to assuage Lou's guilt.

"I don't care what it was. I want to get out of here as soon as possible," says Linda, who is adding panic to her anxiety.

Finally, our rescue sixteen-foot aluminum rowboat with a twenty-five horse-power motor arrives. It's not exactly what we need to get us all out of the grunge, but at least we no longer feel alone. Someone knows we are in trouble and is there to help us escape this mess.

"What the hell did you hit?" he asks first. Not how are you or anyone else hurt, but what did you hit? This response erases that fleeting feeling of comfort at not being alone and getting help.

"We don't know, but it sheared off all the starboard riggers," answers Lou.

"Christ, you sure did a job on the quad," he declares.

"And, we are all okay, thank you," sarcastically from Ann.

He is angry about the damage to the boat, holds us responsible, and doesn't believe that something floating could do this damage. Knowing we are a recreational crew, he is likely not convinced we could row hard and fast enough to do this degree of damage no matter what we hit. Our collective annoyance is quivering at the brink.

"It was my fault," says Lou, "I was bowing. I didn't see a thing."

"Even after we ditched we couldn't see anything, so whatever it was could not have been avoided. It's not Lou's fault," says Linda.

"Whatever, let's get the lightest one of you in the launch."

Lou is the one he wants to take. At first he tries to pull Lou, scraping her chest and belly on the gunnel, but comes within inches of tipping.

"One of you lift her while I pull," he orders as he hangs onto Lou's tank top straps while she twists, kicks, and flops around in the water like a bass caught on a fisherman's hook.

"No, that won't work; let's get to the other side and hang onto the boat. You can lean over and pull her straight up instead of scraping her along the gunnel," states Ann, who is angry at how Peter handles Lou.

At first, Peter is hesitant to lean over but is eventually brave enough to go as far as he needs to get her up and plopped, like that one-hundred-pound bass previously flopping around in the water, onto her belly on one of the seats.

"Okay, you all gather up the riggers and the oars and hand them to Lou and I. Lou, lay them longwise along the seats. Then we will pull the quad alongside and tie one end to the launch, and Lou, you will hang onto the other end as we tow it back to the boathouse," instructs Peter.

It takes another fifteen minutes to gather and untangle all the parts and pieces floating around the scull and load them into the boat. With much effort on everyone's part, we managed to get the quad balanced alongside the launch. And all the while, we are dancing on the muddy bottom, kicking up more crap and trying not to stay in one place long enough to sink to our ankles.

CHAPTER 3

Things That Go Swish in the River

We are so engaged in loading everything up that we neglect to question Peter's decision to leave the three of us in the river while rescuing the shell. Now that they have gone, the consequences of that decision are beginning to sink in.

"That was stupid of him. We could drown out here. He'd be liable," from Linda.

"I suppose we could have argued with the decision," I say.

"Yeah, like we could have won that argument. He knows how expensive those boats are," says Ann.

"Still, it's not a smart decision," says Linda, "especially since I'm having trouble"—her voice volume increases with each word—"keeping my feet from sinking in this muck."

"If he had left the boat here and the oars and taken all four of us, the boat would have drifted, separated from the oars, and we never would have found it all. It makes sense that he left us here," I reason.

"I don't care," says Linda. "I don't like being out here," she shouts at total volume now. "And he didn't even bother to bring us life vests! I can't believe that!"

"Or maybe he had them, and we just forgot to ask him to pitch them to us," I say. "Have we drifted further from shore?"

"Yeah, I think so. Should we do 'rock paper scissors' to see who gets to get up on who's shoulders?" asked Ann, trying to calm Linda.

There is a reason why we don't just crawl out onto land like sane people. At this point in our river, the shores are marshland, inhabited by muskrats, snakes, eels, and gophers, to say nothing of critters that thrive in the sewers. There was not a chance even the bravest of the three of us would venture near that monster-infested wasteland. We are as far from the shoreline as possible and still touch the bottom.

"What's that?" shouts Linda.

"What's what?" from Ann.

"There's something down there. I felt something around my leg. Ah, what is it?" she says as she dances one foot up and then the other, flapping at the murky surface with her hands, trying to keep her feet closer to her body.

"What, what, what is it?" I ask, joining the 'feet off the muddy bottom' dance.

Ann panics next and begins splashing frantically, "What did you feel? Did something bite you?"

"No, I don't know. I'm getting out of here," Linda says, sprinting toward the middle of the river.

"Hey, we should stay together," I say.

"Damn, I'm outta here," shouts Ann taking off after her.

We all start heading farther from the shore, splashing madly, kicking wildly.

"It was a snake," says Linda, breathless from the exertion of the swim. "We've seen them here before."

"Yeah, but that was later in the summer, and besides, they swim above the water with their heads sticking up. We would have seen it," I say.

"So, what? A muskrat, maybe?" asks Ann, gasping for breath as she stops and treads water. "Oooo, uck."

"Don't muskrats have to breathe? They would be on the surface. It couldn't have been a muskrat; it was probably just a fish," I say.

"How can fish live in this crap," cries Ann?

"What else is there?" Linda's voice is now tiny and squeaky.

"Okay, okay, let's not lose our cool here," says Ann. "It was probably just a stick, shoe, or some other gross yuck floating below the surface. It could have been a candy wrapper, a plastic bag, or something your feet stirred out of the muck."

"Or, it could be some other creature that lives in the mud that got kicked up. Or it could be something foul that somebody flushed down the toilet," says a shaky Linda, who then goes on, "It could be an alligator or crocodile, boa constrictor or rattler, or maybe something horrible that all these chemicals have created. It could be, you know. It happens in the sewers of New York. Monsters grow from the crap that people put into the sewers."

"You've been watching too many movies," I say, thinking she must be kidding. "I can't tread water much longer. I have to get where I can touch bottom."

"Oh, god," shouts Linda, "It could be a snapping turtle! Shit!" And with that, she swims out farther.

"Stop, Linda!" I shout. "We need to stay rational here. We've been out in the middle for a few minutes and have felt nothing, but we are beginning to drift downstream because we can't touch the bottom. This river gets deep at some points, and I don't want to drift there. Let's go to the other shore, close enough to touch the bottom. Although, I don't relish the idea of a snapper. They are in these rivers. Shit!"

We all start splashing our way to the other shore.

"You know, if it was a snapper, he was only looking for a couple of toes for breakfast," shouts Ann. "You have plenty to spare."

"Very funny," I say.

"Or maybe it was the sea creature that lurks in the inlet further up river, ooooo," laughs Ann. "Someone spotted something that looked like a giant eel in that inlet on the left just before the bridge."

"Now you are being ridiculous," I say.

"Maybe I just imagined it," says Linda, calming down and trying a forced laugh.

But none of us feel reassured. We've all seen too many Stephen King movies in which everyday situations slowly turn into weird, scary scenarios. And we can't see even an inch below this water's surface. Absolutely anything could lurk there, and we wouldn't know it until it took a bite out of an appendage.

Although the conversation turns back to reliving the actual event of the collision and conjecturing over what in the heck we might have hit, we continue to worry about what slimy, hungry creature could be weaving in and around our legs or scuttling into the mud at our feet preparing to attack.

We try to remain composed, but we are working to minimize the opportunity for anything we can't see to touch our stretched-out legs. So we slow-hop, alternating legs, up and down on the bottom, bending slightly forward with the effort, looking like mimes quietly approaching for a sneak attack.

"Wait!" shouts Linda. "Look. There's a fishing boat." With that, she starts to wave her arms, call, and bounce up and down in the water. "Hey, over here!"

Soon, we all chime in with shouts and bounces, and Ann blows into the whistle she wears around her neck. The boat sees us and heads in our direction.

A middle-aged man motors up next to us in his small aluminum boat with a teenager, a dog, and two fishing poles resting against the gunnels. The dog is excited to see us, if panting, pacing, barking, and tail wagging are any indication.

"What the heck are you three doing out here?" the fisherman asks.

"We had an appointment with our crack dealer, and he took our money and dumped us into the river," I respond.

We tell him our tale of woe, and he volunteers to take us to our dock. But he can only take one with him on the first trip. He will take one of us, leave her, the dog, and his son at our dock, and return for the other two. We gleefully tell him that's just grand.

We decide that Linda is the one who needs to get out of the water and calm down.

The fisherman, whose name is Jack, says, "Okay, Jimmy," to the kid in the boat. "I want you to sit on the other side of the boat and take that damn dog with you. I should be able to pull her in if you two can give her a boost from the bottom," directed at us.

Linda is busy being deferential and mumbling, "I don't want to leave you two here. I can stay. I'll be fine. Why doesn't someone else go."

Ann and I are closing in on Linda, Jack is leaning over the side, and Jimmy is leaning out as far as he can on the other side of the boat.

"One, two, three," shouts Jack, and as we lift her, he grabs her under the arms and pulls, but the damn dog, whose name we learn in a second is Scooter, breaks free from Jimmy and rushes to Jack's side to see what all the commotion is about.

"Scooter, get away!" Jack shouts, holding Linda, but he cannot get the excited, barking, prancing dog out of the way enough to pull her in.

"Scooter, get back here!" yells Jimmy, tugging at his happily wagging tail.

"Get the dog out of the way!" yells Ann. "We can't hold her here forever," she shouts as Linda splashes and thrashes half in and half out of the water.

Scooter is busily leaning out over the water at Jack's side, feet on the gunnel, tongue lolling, panting excitedly, and wagging his entire backside.

"What's he doing?" Linda yells. "Damn dog is drooling on my head!"

Scooter is drooling on Linda's head, absolutely beside himself with glee at this new game.

We hear, "Scooter, here!" The dog disappears. Then we hear a splash, and the boat tilts toward us. Jack drops Linda back into the water and falls to the bottom of the boat.

"Jesus, Jimmy, I told you to hang onto the damn dog!" he shouts. "I almost fell in. Jimmy? Jimmy?" Jack hasn't noticed that his son is in the water in the confusion.

Scooter is panting again over the side, but now at this new game Jimmy invented. Jimmy is thrashing around in the water at the other side of the boat, having fallen backward, when Scooter pranced onto his chest while leaning out for ballast.

"Dammit, Jimmy, what the hell happened to you? How did you get in there? You okay?" Jack asks. "That damn dog!"

"Come to the stern and see if you can climb up the engine shaft. I'll give you a hand," says Jack, mumbling curses to himself.

Linda is beginning to laugh, and Ann and I are already hysterical.

"I'm not going to be able to get into that boat while that damn dog is in there," says Linda. "He's like a Great Dane puppy. He could probably tip that boat over by himself. Incredible."

"Could you see what happened?" asks Ann.

"Yeah, the damn dog jumped on Jimmy, and Jimmy went over backward. I'm amazed the dog didn't go with him," Linda says.

"One, two, three, up," says Jack as Jimmy hikes one foot onto the propeller shaft, one arm around the engine, and one hand pulled by Jack.

Jimmy is okay and laughing, and the dog is deliriously happy again.

"Maybe I can get up at the stern as Jimmy did," says Linda, who is most likely embarrassed that she could not be hauled out of the water as quickly as our lightweight Lou.

"You can try, but you have to be pretty handy, and there is more opportunity to get hurt if you fall onto the prop. Let's try this again to see if we can get Scooter out of the way. I think we can get you up," says Jack. "Tie that damn dog up, or I'll throw him in the river, Jimmy."

Jimmy ties Scooter to the boat's bow, where he cries and jumps in frustration at being left out of all the fun. The team prepares to try again.

"Okay, everyone ready?" asks Jack. "One, two and three."

Jimmy leans out, Jack leans over, and two of us hoist Linda up; she gets about waist high and tries to scramble into the boat. She's hanging over the gunnel just above her belly. Jack has feet planted on either side of her, pulling at her arms, and the boat begins to tip precariously.

Jack says, "Okay, fall back in, and let's try again," as he lets go of Linda.

"I think if we can give her a bigger hoist and do it all together on a count, we can get her in," says Ann.

"The diet is definitely on the immediate horizon. This is so embarrassing. Maybe one of you should try. This is getting ridiculous," says Linda.

"No, we are going to get it this time, Linda," I say. I promise. Besides, you have to go because you are the one who lost a sock. No one should have to have feet in this muck without a sock."

I should explain here that Linda, as one of the quad's powerhouses, is a bit heavier than Lou's one hundred pounds. She is built like a wide, round, and solid fireplug from shoulder to hip. Lifting and pulling her into this boat is not light work. We are beginning to have doubts.

On the next attempt, Jimmy leans out, Jack leans over, and Scooter is now howling at his inability to participate; we hoist her up, but this time as soon as she gets chest high, we plant all hands on her butt, thighs, legs, feet, whatever we can find, and push for all we are worth. Linda lands belly first on Jack, apologizing profusely but in the boat.

The four of us hoot and holler our victory while she gasps for breath. Scooter is untied and begins to lick his greeting and climb over his new best friend, fresh from the river.

Jack says, "I'll be back for you as soon as I can." He starts the motor and heads off to the boathouse.

CHAPTER 4

Monsters of the Deep

"I'm exhausted. Now that I think about it, I don't know how you and I will ever get into Jack's or Peter's boat." Then, with a look of amazement, she actually slaps her forehead before shouting, "I know what's been bugging me about all this. Peter plans to come back to get us, but why didn't he just call the Coast Guard to rescue us? What a jerk. Here, let me get 911," she says as she opens and unlocks the cellphone from its waterproof case around her neck. "What a jerk," she repeats.

"Hello? Hi, there are two people stranded on the Christina River, and we need you to contact the Coast Guard," she continues to iterate our location and our situation.

I'm laughing now. "I can't believe we were all so stupid not to think of that since we've been out here. And how long has it been, anyway, two hours or more?"

"I don't have a watch on, but it has to have been a couple of hours anyway, given all we have done while in the water. We loaded up the launch, got Lou in, almost got eaten by the river creature, hailed a fisherman, loaded Linda in, and here we are," says Ann.

"Yeah, here we are down to two. It seems lonely all of a sudden. I guess there is comfort in numbers, and our numbers are diminishing. Promise me you won't leave me here alone no matter what," I say.

"Promise," says Ann. "Once again, we forgot to ask about life vests."

"I doubt he would have had any anyway. I guess we are back to bouncing up and down on the bottom. Do you have both your socks on?" I ask.

"No, I lost mine near the shore. That was probably what Linda felt drifting along her leg."

"Yeah, I lost mine, too. It sure is quiet out here. Have you ever read reports of anything being flushed down the sewers in Wilmington?" I ask.

"I don't think so, but it wouldn't surprise me. What do people do with all those pythons, baby crocs, rattlers that they get tired of or can't feed or get too big? They probably don't kill them. After all, they are pets," says Ann.

I feel something flow past my leg, but I don't say anything. I keep very still. Ann is still talking about reptilian pets and flushing them down the toilet. I'm waiting to see if I feel it again. Yes, there. And there. Oh, shit. What do I do? If I move, it will bite me. If I don't move, then what? And wait. Where is it? Wait.

"What's wrong?" Ann asks after a minute or two of my nonresponsive silence.

"I don't know," I say very quietly. "Something is swimming around my legs, and I'm afraid to move."

"Is it still there? Can you still feel it?"

"I don't know. Not just now," I say.

"Keep still. It will go away."

"But I'm sinking into the mud," I cry.

"It's okay. Stay calm. You can't sink far."

"But I'm already over the top of my foot, Ann. What should I do?" I'm starting to panic now.

"Okay, take one foot out and walk toward me; here, hold my hand."

"I'm scared," I say as I lift one foot out of the muck and plant it toward Ann. I let go of her hand, lift the other one, and start thrashing through the water, putting as much distance between me and where I was as fast as possible. Ann follows.

We both stop, panting.

"Enough of this fucking river. ENOUGH!" Ann shouts. "We are staying right here until the Coast Guard comes, right here, together."

That's when we hear the engine sound coming at top speed, looking like a cruise ship compared to our little sixteen-foot aluminum rowboat rescuers.

"They must have been down at the port to get here so quickly. Oh, god bless them," I say.

The Coast Guard boat is equipped with little luxuries like a ladder, which avoids our embarrassment of being yanked out of the water to the grunts and groans of these Coast Guard uniformed men. And while they ask how we came to be standing near the river's shoreline, up to our ankles in mud on this lovely sunny summer day, they are not at all critical of our tale and do not laugh at us. And, best of all, they do not have a dog aboard.

We thank them profusely as they hand us towels to dry off, and we head to our boathouse. It doesn't matter that they are balding and wrinkled. We love them for rescuing us from the muck and the unnamed horror of the river monsters.

Ann asks what animals are in the river and receives the usual list of suspects from these experts.

"Have you ever heard of anything weird, like crocs, boas, or anything else?" she asks. "You know, like in the sewers of New York."

Our heroes deny any knowledge of such anomalies in our town, but she tries to convince them that something nasty and unknown is lurking in the yucky depths.

"Well, one of us felt something creepy near that shore, and then another felt something slithering . . ." she begins.

CHAPTER 5

Living the Tall Tale

A few days later, two rowers from our quad motored out to the incident scene to see if they could spy the offending object. They found a huge log stuck in the mud close to the shore, with a broad limb rising a foot above the water's surface at low tide and completely hidden when the tide was high.

The offending tree limb was named "The Cobra." In subsequent emails to club members, the location and description of the cause of one of the club's favorite quads being in "sick bay" were referenced by this name. For weeks, the tale of Predator (the name of our quad) Meets Cobra was embellished as it circulated through the club, and the incident became referred to as the Titanic Affair.

Several members questioned whether riggers could be sheared off by some stuck in the mud tree limb. One member, who lashes out by email at everyone about everything, especially when he has less than a full complement of information and a few glasses of wine, insisted the crew must have crashed the scull into a bridge.

This suspicion of crew incompetence, although not warranted this time, of course, was expected since crews never step up to blame when it comes to damaging boats. There is nothing worse in the lexicon of rowing than to be judged incompetent on the water. So, all manner of incredible scenarios have been cooked up by crews to avoid admitting they made a mistake. The Cobra sounded like another of these improbable stories.

Eventually, the drama died, and the crew's version of the event was accepted. But primarily, this was accomplished by the diversion of remembering and retelling other crew's tall rowing tales.

There was one about a collegiate men's medal-winning eight, who, macho as they were, were caught in a sudden storm and expeditiously swamped by twenty-five mile-per-hour gusts. Eights never go over unless someone does something stupid. In this case, the excuse was raging "perfect storm" conditions with ocean-size swells and pelting rains on the fifty-yard-wide Christina River. We all listened intently to the story as it was told by the crew, shaking our heads in total disbelief at this fantastic, never-before-seen storm. In private, our eyes rolled as we conjectured about who on the crew screwed up big enough for the boat to go over.

Another tale remembered was of a coach driving a launch who fell out of the boat while the motor stayed engaged and circled her. The club's motor was fitted with a safety dead switch, which the coaches should clip to their clothing when driving the launches alone. If a coach should fall out of the boat, the cord attached to their clothing will pull a switch that turns the motor off. Being assured by this coach that she had done what she was supposed to and clipped the dead switch to her jacket, plenty of money, time, and effort was expended to refit all motors with new switches. Coaches still don't use the dead switches. It must be a fashion thing.

During that same incident, this coach wore a rain jacket marketed to rowers and personalized with the club and the individual's name embroidered on the breast. Pride of sport, club, and personalized so that no one could walk off with it encouraged many club members to order and wear these jackets while rowing in cold or rainy weather.

In this incident, our coach discovered that if you tied this waterproof rain jacket at the waist and fell into the river, the jacket held water inside and dragged you under the surface like a croc with a kill. An interesting design made specifically for use in water sports.

There was a memorable collision of a quad and a double, leaving both boats in one piece but destroying two sets of oars. Lots of name-calling and jabbering ensued about who should have been on which side of the river and who was not looking where they were going. No one, of course, was really to blame for the incident. The tide was extreme that day, and any crew would have had trouble staying on the correct side of the river and looking behind them for potential disasters. Neither of the bow persons was using the dorky, look-behind-you mirrors or spy glasses. Such is vanity among young rowers.

The tide often has its way with club crews. A quad, rowed by an elite women's racing crew, claimed to be swept by the river's strong current one evening into an old piling, cutting quite a hole in the hull. The piling was part of an old RR bridge each crew rowed past daily. It's not like it popped up out of nowhere, moved, or changed its nature. So it must have been that that nasty tide just slammed that scull right into that old piling. When was the city going to get rid of that hazard anyway?

This same crew repeated this crash one early morning, but the second time, the fog was to blame for not seeing that old piling in the same place as it had been the last time they hit it.

One sweep (eight rowers, one oar each) crew had entered a regatta. They took all the riggers (the things that hold the oarlocks and oars) off the boat to trailer it to the Wye River. The morning of the race, crew members worked nuts and bolts to get the riggers back on the sweep boat to be rowed.

As their turn came up to launch, eight rowers fastened their oars into the oarlocks, climbed into the boat, and tried to row out into the start position on the river. But something was not working correctly. No one could get their oars into and out of the water properly.

The coach, realizing the problem from his position on shore, called the crew back in disgust. The crew disembarked, pulled the boat out of the water, and removed the riggers. Someone had packed the riggers up for transport in a way that encouraged this crew to attach them to the boat backward. It wasn't the crew's fault. Rowers would never make such a stupid mistake.

But the excitement on our river is not always about mistakes for which no one will accept blame. There are just some weird things that are observed and experienced. All manner of things float on our river. A floating baby crib prompted a crew to call the Coast Guard to check it out to ensure no baby was wrapped in the bedding.

Something with four stiff things sticking straight up on the water's surface was a bloated, stiff, dead deer.

Two singles out for a morning row discovered a baseball cap and stopped to fetch it from the water. They found it perched atop a human head, which later turned out to be a missing person.

Lou was rowing when a car toppled off a bridge. She called 911 and stayed with the passengers until they were rescued.

Our club doesn't have a monopoly on experiencing odd things on the water, either. Other clubs have reported some weird phenomena. A feral cat was spied swimming two hundred yards across the Intercoastal in Sarasota, Florida. Five deer swam alongside a scull from the island to land in Mamaroneck, New York.

At some point, you must wonder if a scull looks to another whale like some shiny new friend. A sixty-footer curiously swam thirty feet from a double in Monterey Bay. A baby whale might have been looking for mom when he approached and spouted forty feet from a sweep boat in San Francisco Bay, much to their dismay since the stench from her dead fish breath was overwhelming.

Oars have been boarded by chirping otters. Sculls have been tail-slapped by beavers; boarded by minnows, salmon, and remora; struck repeatedly by sea bass attracted to the shiny hull; and attacked by swans during mating season.

Dolphins have frolicked around sculls in the upper Chesapeake, where they are rarely seen. An enormous moose in Alaska swam beside an eight, trying to get past them. Cow-nosed rays rest on the surface off the Pacific coast and interfere with blade work. A tuckered-out squirrel welcomed a ride on a single after trying to swim across a river in New York.

You never know what jollies a river or bay may have in store for you when out rowing.

CHAPTER 6

In the Beginning

"There's an open house at the Wilmington Rowing Club this weekend," says my darling husband, reading the *News Journal* weekend activities. "You should go down."

"Would you go with me?"

"Yeah, sure. I won't row, but I'll go with you."

I usually would not have considered learning to row, but my sister-in-law (living in Alexandria, Virginia) had become smitten. She was so enamored that she would row every weekday morning at 5:30 to get her row in before work. A schedule like this was not something she would suffer lightly. Addiction? Lunacy? Indeed, some changes in brain chemistry. I was curious enough to give it a go.

On Saturday, we observed a handful of people scurrying about the boathouse, setting up Learn to Row signs and tables. We were frequently hustled out of the way with loud shouts of "heads up" by short people leading rowers carrying boats overhead or resting on shoulders. It was a noisy scene with shouts of "overhead and up," "split to shoulders and down," "one foot in and in," "watch the riggers," and "Waynuf." Such was my introduction to the rowing lingo, necessarily shouted to be heard above the din. There were long boats with eight carriers, shorter ones with four, and some twenty-foot-long singles balanced directly on a rower's head, defying Newton's laws of gravity. It was a hive of bees abuzz, each seeming to understand their role. The scene overwhelmingly bamboozled this naïve, shy, fifty-year-old woman enough to consider walking away without saying a word to anyone.

"Ask someone about the Learn to Row."

"They all seem pretty busy," I shouted, trying to be heard above the cacophony. "I don't need to."

"Just go up to that woman and ask her what the drill is."

My shyness was beginning to make me feel like a five-year-old, so I asked someone, "Uh, I'm here to learn about rowing." It would take four weekends, two hours each Saturday and Sunday morning, and cost $200. She shuffled me the sign-up list, and I was good to go. I had no idea what lay in store.

A month later, I was armed with a swim test signed unintelligibly by a friend who had never seen me swim but claimed, at my request, to be a swim instructor at the local YMCA. Going to the Y and taking the swim test was unnecessary since I knew I could swim. Bedecked with a check for $200, sunglasses, a water bottle, and a sweatband, I arrived at the boathouse. It seemed to be a repeat of the same confusion: boats being carried, shouting, someone trying to get us organized. It was Saturday morning in the summer and a naturally busy time at the house.

"Okay, you are Danielle. And you are Jake. Is that right?" asks an official-looking woman with a clipboard.

"Can I get your swim test and check, please?"

Ten other people showed up, and after almost forty-five minutes of checking everyone off and collecting our money, we were ushered to a hot upstairs room full of rowing machines and shown a safety video by the club's safety officer, Ed. We heard all about the things we should and should not do on the water, which we all promptly forgot. The only thing making a lasting impression was the video of a rower being pushed out of the boat by his oar handle when he did something wrong called "catching a crab." It looked painful and scary, but it had a catchy name.

We were then introduced to the rowing machines. Over time, I have come to think of these as instruments of torture, akin only to the Nordic Track cross-country skiing invention. But they help you become familiar with the sliding seat, stationery shoes, and uncomfortable body positions. When it was my turn to try the machine, I discovered how aerobic rowing is. Hmmm . . . having smoked for many years, my lungs were not exactly pristine. I was having my doubts about this venture.

On Sunday, we were introduced to "the tanks." This is the next step in simulation and familiarization. The tanks consist of two, maybe fifteen by sixty feet, three feet deep, rectangular above-ground dipping pools. These are laid side by side longwise, separated by a two-foot-wide wooden platform. An aerial view might resemble a moth with rectangular wings.

Attached to this central platform are eight sets of stationary shoes. In front of each of these and alternating right and left sides is a rigger, a three-foot-long metal arm designed to hold an oar. It juts out over the water from the sides of the boat. An oarlock is at the end of these metal arms, which does just that. Duh. Behind each set of fixed slanted shoes and rigger is a wooden seat that slides back and forth about three feet on metal rails. I fear it's much too complicated and dangerous to be fun.

To add to my discomfort, the humid air and combination of water and walls that generate echoes transport me to the dreaded high school pool. In those days, a menstrual period was enough to get excused from swim class, and I had mine at swim time every month. I proclaimed to my buddies that I disliked swimming, but it was actually about getting my hair wet. Vain and insecure in my fourteen-year-old skin, I couldn't repair the damage the water did to my fine, flat hair after a swim, making me resemble a cat dipped in a bath. No more fluff. Consequently, I could dog paddle but flubbed an attempt at the standard swim stroke that always resulted in getting water up my nose. But I digress.

Eight of us walk along this "catwalk" between the tanks, gingerly stepping over seats, sliding back and forth on rails, carrying a nine-foot oar. We position ourselves behind the person in front of us and attempt to plant our derrieres on a moving seat. It reminds me of a computer game—site the target, aim your weapon (in this case, butt), and hope to disable the enemy (here, the moving seat.) Oars are splashing into the water next to us as people attempt to keep them balanced and fail. The women are nervously giggling, the men laughing loudly, and it all echoes off the walls of this claustrophobically humid room.

"Hey, at least we can't drown in water this shallow," Jake behind me says.

"Uh, you can drown in a bathtub," I respond sarcastically.

Everyone is nervous. No one knows what to do or how to do it. Just getting into the tanks and in position is remarkably unwieldy. For the second time, I'm questioning the wisdom of my choice to be here.

Our instructor, Kris, begins, "Okay. Everyone settled? Got your feet in the shoes?"

"The shoes are too big," a woman my age, two people behind me, reports.

Kris gives us a you've-got-to-be-kidding-me look, hands on hips, legs spread, sighs, and says, "Shoes never fit because lots of rowers with different size feet use them. It doesn't make a difference. Next week when we get into a boat, bring socks. Women might bring a pair of thicker socks so the shoes won't seem so large. If your feet are small enough, you can try wearing water shoes inside them. Everyone wears socks because other rowers use the same shoes, and most of us would like to avoid athlete's foot or warts."

Lovely, I think as I look at my sockless feet, wondering what dirty little teenager wore these before me. "Why didn't they tell us that yesterday?" I say to Jake over my shoulder.

"Yeah," he agrees.

Here we all are, barefooted, squirming in our seats, wiggling our toes, trying not to think of the horrible tropical disease the last person to use these shoes blessed us with.

Kris, who is five foot four and probably weighs 110 pounds, brooks no nonsense from this group. "Okay, let's learn how to put our oars into the oarlocks and secure them in place. You do not want them to come out of the oarlock once you are on the water."

We spend the next hour splashing each other mercilessly, failing badly at pulling the seat up with our feet or pushing back with our legs in tandem. At this point, the notion of coordinating these efforts with the correct movement of oar blades into and out of the water is clearly beyond us. By the end of the two hours, I'm sweaty, exhausted, and already sore—and we aren't even on the water yet.

CHAPTER 7

Sweep Rowing.
Where's the Broom?

It's now the second weekend of Learn to Row, and most of us return, not yet dismayed. The woman complaining that the shoes didn't fit her last week is absent. Either she had a previous engagement, is tied up in some emergency, or has a fetish about her ill-fitting shoes.

Jake, my now buddy, is here, and I learn he's a hiker. We are sharing stories of places we've hiked and plan to hike when our safety officer who showed us that dreadful video of a rower doing a backflip into the water after "catching a crab" shows up with a friendly, "Hi, how are ya?"

"My work with you guys is finished. I'm here to row. Enjoy yourselves, and remember what I taught you last week," he says as he disappears inside the boathouse.

Kris introduces our small assemblage to Fred, our coach. Fred is medium height, with salt-and-pepper hair, wiry, and all muscle. His suntanned, weathered, wrinkled face is the only thing that dates him. I'd guess his age is fifty-something.

"We are lucky to have Fred as our club's coach. He is very experienced, has won many medals and trophies, and just last year won in the single scull category at Nationals," Kris, our instructor, tells us.

We all murmur, "Wow," as we try to figure out what a scull and Nationals are, and Fred smiles sheepishly.

"Okay, we need to get gear for the coach," Kris says.

She explains that we must carry a small aluminum launch down to the water, fit it with a twenty-five horse-power motor, and add a megaphone, seat cushion, lifejacket, gas tank, and safety bag of goodies for the coach to use during our lesson.

"You four, stay with Fred, and he will show you how to get the oars," she says. "The rest of you come with me."

As we carry the launch down to the dock, some brave newbie asks Kris, "What is a scull?"

"There are two kinds of rowing," she says. "In the first, each person in the boat has just one oar. This is called sweep rowing. This is what you are learning."

Regardless of its *nom de plume*, sweep rowing does not resemble the sweeping motion. Where the hell did the name come from, I'm thinking?

"The other form is sculling, in which each person in the boat manages two oars."

"Sweep rowing can be done with eight rowers, four, or even two. Most sweep rowers row in an eight, like the boat you will use. Another difference is that sweep boats have a coxswain," she continues. "I'm going to be your coxswain."

"So what does a coxswain do exactly?" asks a thirty-something guy whose name, I think, is Maurice.

"A good coxswain is a bossy small person with a huge voice," says coach Fred, who has been following us down the ramp to the water. She's coach, helmsman, and psychologist all rolled into one. A good one, like Kris, prods a crew to regatta victory, screaming things at her crew like 'Come on, you a bunch of dickheads, show me some power,' or 'You going to let those pansies pass you,'" he laughs. She gives him a feigned, dirty look. Later, we learn they are a "thing."

"And she/he has to be tiny," he adds. Otherwise, she/he won't fit into the coxswain's space on a boat that is only about eighteen inches wide.

"That's the only reason I started coxing in the first place," she says. "My real love is rowing."

"The sport produces lots of rowers but few coxswains. Occasionally, a rower volunteers to take a turn coxing and clearly does not remember about the tight quarters. We get them out, but not without embarrassment and lots of chuckles," jokes Fred. With enough things in life that are out of my control to be embarrassed about, I vowed never to volunteer to cox. Ever!

Kris led us back up to the boathouse after we put the launch into the water and outfitted it for Fred. She took us to a monster yellow, heavy wooden boat with a smooth, round bottom. Although it is upside down on a rack, we can see that it is sixty feet long and two feet wide, narrowing to points at both ends. When our nine-foot oars are attached, we will look to the air force pilots overhead like a giant yellow caterpillar with four legs on a side.

"You will sit in the seat I assign you, facing away from the boat's direction. For today, I will decide if you row port or starboard. I will be sitting in the back of the boat, facing you and the direction the boat is headed," she says. "Since I'm the only one who can see where we are going, you now know enough to be nice to me," she laughs and raises her eyebrows. "Your fate is in my hands. And one other thing: I am your coxswain, and coxswains rule always. You are to do whatever I tell you immediately and without question. There is only one boss of this boat, and it's me! Got it?"

We all shake our heads in agreement, having no idea what she might tell us to do.

"This boat is about three hundred pounds and has to be carried overhead from here down the ramp to the water where we just put the launch. You will each be required to carry your share. It's heavy. We don't allow cheaters.

There are nine of us here today, and Ed will help you carry, so that will lighten the load a little for the first time," Kris tells us.

"The most important thing about carrying the boat down to the water is doing exactly what Kris tells you," Ed reiterates. "It doesn't matter if you think it doesn't make sense. She is responsible for your safety; someone can get hurt if you don't do what she tells you."

"All right, already we got the message," I'm muttering. "Let's just get this whale down to the water."

Kris reviewed some of the commands with us and told us she and Fred would walk alongside the boat as we carried it to be sure we all knew what to do.

I'm feeling scared and nervous. Probably everyone is.

"Lay hold," she shouts. Nine of us and Ed lean under our long, yellow sweep boat, which looks like a giant banana. It rests upside down on a rack a little more than head height. We tuck our heads inside the boat's cavity and grab its edges.

"And up," the boss commands." We lift the monster banana overhead.

Over the years since those lessons, I have calculated that three hundred pounds divided by eight rowers results in each rower handling only thirty-eight pounds or so. This is a nominal amount for almost anyone fit. However, I've learned that many recreational rowers have bad backs, shoulders, sore necks, arms, flat feet, PMS, a hangover, and other sundry maladies. These dreaded rowing mates don't lift their fair share. And in some cases, I've been convinced they are hanging onto the boat for support. I'm constantly craning my neck to see if everyone's feet are solidly on the ground. All you can do is hope the march to the water is quick.

"Out of the house and watch the riggers on the doors," she says. Fred quietly coaches us to move inches right or left so the riggers, like three-foot daggers jutting out on either side of the boat, don't bang into the boathouse door jams.

Lest you think this doesn't happen, I have watched crews hit door jams, trees, peoples' heads, other boats, runners along the riverwalk, bikers, and so forth. Since the boat is carried a good four or five feet off the ground, children and animals are not usually among the casualties.

"Waynuf." This mysterious phrase means "stop dead" in rowing code, but no one knows where it comes from or how to spell it.

"Split to shoulders and down." This means that half of the crew duck their heads out from under the boat they have been carrying overhead and lower it to rest on their right shoulder, and four duck their heads out on the opposite side and drop it to their left shoulder in a supposedly synchronized move.

Fred told each of us which way to go as we carried the boat out of the house. Subsequently, I learned that it could be a moment of confusion unless a crew rows together routinely or remembers to decide which shoulder each will choose ahead of time.

If six rowers, for instance, choose to go out on one side, leaving two to hold the entire weight of the other side, a great deal of yelling and screaming from the two holding one whole side ensues as the boat tilts precariously while the six on the other side squabble about who should switch sides, sounding a bit like excited chickens in a hen house when the rooster shows up.

Down to the water's edge we trudge—groaning, puffing, and moving as fast as we dare with three hundred pounds on our shoulders, anxious to end this grinding pain.

At the dock, Kris shouts, "Overhead and up." With our last modicum of energy, we all lift the boat over our heads again, parallel to the side of the dock.

"Toe to the edge," she commands. We point one foot toward the edge of the dock in what looks to be one-half of ballet's third position, if I recall correctly.

"And roll it." We roll the boat, bottom side down, push it away from the dock, and lay it on the water, delighted to be free of the overwhelming weight.

We all take a big breath with the boat finally in the water.

"Okay, Ed will hold the boat for us. Everyone come over here to the oars," says Kris.

Fred has a piece of paper with him, and he calls out our names and which seat we will be in. "Janet bow, Maurice two seat, Danielle three seat, Jake four, Allison five and Nancy six. Alana and George, you will ride with me in the launch, and we will switch out halfway through the row so you can get into the boat."

"We have Marie and Mark here today to row our stroke and seven seat for us. The goal is to get all eight of you in the boat by yourselves. For now, experienced rowers serve as your training wheels to keep you out of the water," he says.

"As you know, there are oars for the port side and oars for the starboard side. They are not the same. So, be careful to choose the right one," he tells us.

"Oh, god," I mumble to Allison, standing next to me, "one more thing to remember."

"Yeah," she says. "Speaking of that, do you remember when the blades are supposed to go into the water?"

"Listen up," shouts Fred, who then shows us which oar to use on which side. Thank god they are color-coded.

"Okay, grab your oar, find your seat, and stand beside it," says Fred.

"How do I know which one is three seat?" I ask Kris.

"It's the third seat from the front of the boat," she answers. As I look from the bow to stern in puzzlement, she puts a hand on her hip while bending one knee, gives a how-can-you-be-so-stupid smirk, and points to the bow.

"Oh, thanks."

Once we have fastened our oars into the oarlocks to Kris's satisfaction, she says, "Okay, now we will learn to adjust the shoes."

Although the shoes are fixed to the boat, they can be adjusted to accommodate short and tall rowers. Positioned for difficult access, wingnuts can be loosened, and the shoes slide farther from or closer to the sliding seat.

We are told that these can usually be turned by hand, but occasionally, some macho guy tightens a wingnut down, and no one can loosen it. Kris introduces us to the nonregulation device known affectionately as "the Woody."

"It's not always made of wood and isn't used on anything wooden, so the name is a mystery. You can't buy them anywhere. We make them," she tells us. "They always work to loosen the wingnut."

So the boat is in the water, the appropriate oars are in the oarlocks, and the shoes are adjusted to each rower's height. Water bottles are thrown into the bottom of the boat, shoes removed and stowed on the dock; Kris is seated up front with a microphone in front of her mouth as those of us on the right stand holding port oars in our soggy stocking feet (the dock is invariably wet), ready for our next instruction.

It is a fact learned by every rower early in their training that rowing requires ultimate synchronization. These boats are round on the bottom, have no keel, and have no means of staying upright on the water on their own. They must be held at the dock so they don't swamp while rowers get all the paraphernalia attached and loaded.

"Port oars out," Kris shouts. All rowers with an oar on the right side slide it through the oarlock until it catches on the collar, leaving about three feet inside the oarlock. No, this is not a mistake. The port is on the rower's right because sculls are rowed backward. Thought you had me there, didn't you?

"One foot in," she calls. Each rower puts one socked foot in front of the sliding seat with the other on the dock. It has been drilled into us that no one may ever lay a foot on the bottom of the boat. They are made of such material that a foot will penetrate the hull, rendering the boat useless and out of commission for a costly repair.

"And in." The protocol here is to perform a one-legged squat on the leg already in the boat and attempt to hit the sliding seat (typically anywhere but under where you want to sit) with your butt and pull your other leg into the boat. You can use your hands on the gunnels (side of the boat) to slow the descent. Thank god for little favors.

We wiggle to adjust our now-lowered butts squarely on that sliding seat, move our feet out in front of us, waggle them into the no-fit shoes, and try to immobilize our feet by tightening the Velcro strap on the shoes.

The coxswain yells, "Count down when ready." Each rower, beginning with a bow seat, yells their seat number, indicating they have made their butt adjustments, tied their shoes, has hold of their oar, and is ready to worry about balancing the boat on open water.

"One hand on the dock and shove." We shove away from the dock and are finally underway, hoping the row is joyous enough that we will forget we have to do all this in reverse when we return.

CHAPTER 8

Not My Bad

One of the most annoying things about sweep rowing is the "hurry up and wait" shuffle.

Let me set this stage for you. Remember that rowing a sweep boat takes eight rowers and one coxswain. Recreational sweep rowers are adults, at least chronologically, between mostly forty and sixty. These middle-aged rowers support themselves by performing some paid contribution (job) to society. Most, but not all, choose to perform this paid contribution during daylight hours.

This profile means that nine people must leave their place of employment when their workday ends, no matter what emergency confronts them. They climb into their cars, become tangled in rush hour traffic, arrive at the boathouse hauling their rowing togs and water bottles in some satchel and clanking their heels or wingtips on the concrete, and change as quickly as possible before presenting themselves to the rest of the crew. By the time they join the swelling numbers, they are out of breath and carrying a full measure of anxiety from their stressful day and guilt at rushing out the door at work.

Here's a typical scenario: The crew has agreed to meet at 5:30. It's 5:40, and there are four or five rowers assembled, others having been unavoidably waylaid by a marauding boss, anxious employee, or last-minute call from an elusive client.

At 5:45, one of the crew joins the gathering and asks, "So how many do we have so far?"

Someone will do a head count, "I think we are up to six."

"Who are we missing?"

"I'm not sure who's scheduled to row tonight."

When the coxswain arrives, she asks, "So, who's here?"

Someone in the group will tick off the six wandering around the house, who are attempting to decompress while waiting for the last rower to arrive.

Ten more minutes pass, the row is now delayed twenty minutes, and the once-happy group of seven is now grumpy as a car in low gear going uphill, groaning and whining. Some have angered their bosses, abandoned their colleagues, broken speed limits, run stop signs, and turned right on red when the sign clearly says not to, all to be here on time. For their efforts, they have been left to shuffle around, waiting on other crew members.

"It's Joan who's not here." Or Tom or Sally or Jan.

"I'm sure she said she would be here. She replied to the email yesterday."

It's about that time that the phone rings. It is, in fact, Joan. The stories vary and are not terribly creative: stuck in traffic, the kid is sick, looked too much like rain, forgot to throw rowing clothes in the car, has a GI issue, flat tire or feels a psychotic episode coming on, broke a nail, the dog ate my rowing socks, or some other real or imagined excuse for not showing up.

It's inevitable. It's nine people. As often as 30 percent of the time, someone doesn't make it, and eight people are left to shuffle all that anxiety, compounded now with the frustration of hurrying up and waiting. Oops, I fooled you. We won't row after all.

But even getting onto the water does not guarantee the crew will go home satisfied. The entire crew in attendance is just the first hurdle. Remember that a sweep boat has a rounded bottom. As such, the boat is unbalanced, tipping from side to side. So, an essential part of a good row is what we call a good "set." This means that each rower is balanced well enough that the boat stays even in the water. Sound easy? It's not.

An essential part of a good rowing technique is holding each oar at a hand level inside the boat such that the blades are just above the water's surface between strokes. Just below the boobs is one suggestion for placement of those hands. This falls apart if the boat is being rowed by women over sixty whose boobs are heading toward their knees or by rowers who are substantially different in height. Placement of that oar handle then becomes more of a feel than an exact science. And if even one person on the crew doesn't get that feel for where it should be, the boat lists to one side.

Another factor affecting the boat's balance is how deeply each rower digs into the water. Instinct from our rowboat days tells us that the deeper we drop our blade, the further we move. But sweep rowing is different. It is best done when the blade is not quite fully covered, and the oars are drawn straight back and not dug deep.

There is also the leaning problem. Rowers need to stay centered to keep the boat balanced. Some people inexplicably develop a habit of leaning to one side. An error made by just one person on any of these issues can cause the boat to be uncomfortably unbalanced.

A small list is tolerable. Experienced rowers are good enough to adjust to one rower's slightly different technique, but I've been in some boats where that is not correctable. What happens is that rowers on the upside of the listing side cannot get their oars anywhere near the water. They subsequently engage in air stroking.

On the downside of a listing boat, things are worse. Rowers cannot get their oars out of the water. This is the more uncomfortable of the two sides. Arms, shoulders, and backs are wrenched, jerked, and twisted into unnatural positions to move oars through and out of the water. None of this is good for a crew's body or mood.

The standard fix for severe listing is letting two rowers stop rowing and balance the boat by keeping their oars flat on the water. This sign of defeat is a last resort only acted upon when a coxswain is frustrated or concerned that the boat may roll over and dump her and her crew into the disgusting river. This training wheel plan prevents any disasters of this sort but deflates the crew's confidence and ego.

A crew inexperienced enough to need two rowers to fill in as training wheels frequently runs into another quirk of novice rowers, catching a crab. Most new rowers think this phrase is way cool. They can be overheard asking each other after a row, "Did you catch a crab," with a slight lilt and a big grin. With glee, they go home at night and tell their families they "caught a crab today," laughing at the cute phrase and feeling very rowerly about it all.

To experienced rowers, catching crabs is about as amusing as seeing the kind that comes with a one-night stand. The act occurs when a rower cannot get their oar out of the water at the end of the stroke, virtually bringing the row to a dead stop. The danger, real or imagined, is that the forward motion of the boat propels the oar so tightly to the side of the shell and with such force that, in the process, the rower is knocked off their cute little derriere into a backward double gainer, out of the boat and into the water in milliseconds. At least, that is what our safety officers would have us believe. Personally, I don't think even a powerful crew, much less recreational rowers, could ever move fast enough in the water to generate such force.

Much like mature consenting adults, experienced rowers would never be caught catching a crab. In an experienced recreational boat, everyone considers themselves a skilled rower. Many recreational rowers have been successful racers in their youth and remind themselves each day with a sigh and a glance at a dresser mirror festooned with college medals.

If an experienced crew cannot balance the boat, they will search for the guilty party. The conversation at the bar after such a row goes a little like this.

A gulp of beer and a big sigh," That was the worst row. I couldn't keep my oar off the water!"

"Yeah, Fran was going too deep again."

"I noticed Joyce's left shoulder was raised too. That put us down on port."

"Who was that behind you?"

"Uh, oh yeah, that was Linda. Why?"

"She was rushing the slide [rowing talk for sliding the seat up faster than everyone else]. She was in front of me Monday, and I almost lost it. I kept telling her to slow the slide. Worked for five minutes, and then she was right back at it. God, I hate that," complained Mary.

"Does it drive anyone else to distraction that Rose counts every stroke out loud? What's that all about?"

"Hey, you were behind me, right?"

"Yeah, I was in two seat."

"Did it look to you like I was going too deep?"

"No, not at all. You looked great."

A worried look crosses her face, and she whispers, "I sometimes have a problem following stroke at the catch [placing the oar into the water]."

Reassuringly, "You're a great rower. It's Georgiana who's never in sync with the feather [the preparation of the oar to enter the water, which MUST be done by everyone simultaneously]."

They continue to pick apart the rest of the crew while they pat themselves on the back for being good rowers. After all, they have dust-encrusted racing medals on those mirrors at home to prove it.

For a couple of years, the sweep rec crew included a few rowers everyone loved to hate who took the brunt of all the blame for bad rows.

Roxy was an ex-ballerina and fancied herself just a cut above everyone else. She would wrap her dancer calves in loose ACE bandages to protect their delicate skin from banging against the seat rails and creating black and blue marks. Some rowers covet these bruises as a badge of serious rowing power. Others, mysteriously, don't bang their calves. Is it poor rowing technique or fat calves? Roxy was a banger, but she could not tolerate bruises on her precious calves, so she donned these raggedy, old, and well-used ACE bandages.

She would arrive early and stretch out before her row while the rest were involved in the sweep "hurry up and wait shuffle." Her stretching exercises were designed for dancing, done slowly, sensuously, with poise, nose in the air, toes pointed. She performed for us, showing us her incomparable skills. We were striving to be good rowers, not ballerinas. This behavior did not endear her to the rest of the crew. She was not a good rower and often spoiled the row for the rest of her crew.

Marcy had another problem: her attire. Rowers dress is not always flattering, but spandex is necessary, for reasons we will explore later. Since it can be uncomfortably revealing, rowers are careful to cover up until they get to the boathouse and some are even considerate enough to wait to strip down until they get into the boat. But none, except Marcy, dared to show up in the parking lot and parade past shops and businesses on her way to the boathouse in her sports bra.

It might not have been an issue if Marcy had been twenty and buff or even forty and taut. But she was over fifty and no longer sported an athlete's body. That space between the bra bottom and spandex waistband sported several rolls of fifteen pounds of fat gained, lost, gained back again, lost, and permanently gained back more unruly than ever—rolls of fat that inevitably peek out over the waistbands of pants no matter what new product is devised to keep them hidden, rolls of fat resplendent with the dreaded pockmarks of cellulite.

Shop clerks next to our boathouse called to complain about the scantily clad older rowers, but no one could figure out how to approach the subject with Marcy graciously.

And most unfortunate for Marcy, she was a lousy rower. No matter how often she rowed or how much she was coached on her poor technique, she did not improve. Most of us cringed when she showed up in her cottage cheese midriff, knowing the row would suck. Not much left to redeem her in the crew's eyes.

Carol didn't seem to like anyone, including the coach. She complained constantly about other rowers' inadequacies and the workout's difficulty for an over-fifty-something woman.

She found very creative excuses for not being able to row her best: she was given an inferior oar or the ripple on the water spoiled her stroke, the shoes didn't fit, the woman in front of her wore a distracting design on the back of her T-shirt, the smell of French fries from the local restaurant reminded her of how hungry she was, the seagulls on the river ruined her concentration, to name a few.

She complained of perceived neglect by other crew members, which was real by this time. Some ache or ailment always thwarted her ability to carry the boat. We were routinely held up, even after the hurry up and wait shuffle, while she found some unsuspecting member of another crew to carry her share of the boat for her.

We might have forgiven Marcy's appearance if she had been a good rower. We could have accepted Carol if she had been friendly and a good sport. But in her case, we found nothing to like. And Roxy was just a pain in every way. We gradually eased each of these women off the crew. But they did nicely serve to catch the blame for all the bad rows we experienced for a couple of seasons, saving the rest of us from admitting any failing.

CHAPTER 9

Pink Panthers on the Water

Several of us were at the boathouse one early spring performing the annual winter maintenance. A handful of rec rowers were lollygagging around, getting reacquainted and catching up on lives lived since the season's close.

Lou said, "Hey anyone up to take out a quad tomorrow night around 5:30?"

I was standing nearby and responded with, "Sure. Who else can we get?"

"I'll go out with you as long as I don't have to bow," said Linda.

"I'll be happy to bow," says Lou.

Overhearing us, Ann adds, "Are you guys going out tomorrow? I can go out if you don't mind me joining you."

"Of course not," says Linda, "if it's okay with everyone else."

"Fine with me."

"Great," adds Lou.

We vaguely knew each other but had never rowed together. We hadn't a clue about how it would go, but we were decidedly anxious to get onto the water, so we were willing to take a chance. I harbored substantial doubts the row would be stellar because we were so physically mismatched. Lou was tiny, Ann was tall, and Linda and I were average. Such differences usually don't make the greatest choice for decent crews. But we were all recreational rowers, had many years of experience, and figured, how bad it could be? All we had to do was hold the balance (keep the boat "set") and not roll over.

The first good sign was that we were all on time in the afternoon; Lou bowed (the seat that controls where we go and how fast we get there), I stroked (the seat in the stern that sets the rate of rowing whom everyone else has to follow), and we kept Ann and Linda, our powerhouses, in the middle. We amazed ourselves by being set, having a good workout, and having more than a few good laughs. It was great. We vowed to go out again a few days later. And that was that.

Did I forget to mention rec crews frequently invent names for themselves? We had a novice sweep crew that called itself the Motleys, for obvious reasons, an older men's eight (that can't get no satisfaction) known as the Rowing Stones, and an older ladies' eight who unabashedly referred to themselves as the Hot Flashes.

We became known as the Pink Panthers.

We had many good laughs and adventures over the years. Not the least was when we sheared off all four riggers and ended up swimming the river, battling the monsters below the murky surface of the Christina River, and enduring three rescues, including a fishing boat fiasco.

The first year we rowed together, the crew decided they wanted to do the head race (a timed 5,000-meter race) on our river. I was out of town on business, so they needed to find a replacement stroke. Lou had rowed doubles a few times with an equally tiny Louisa, another active recreational rower in our club, who was willing to stroke in the race. According to Lou, Louisa's stroke rate depended entirely upon how upsetting her day was. The more unsettling the day, the faster the stroke.

It might seem logical that a fast stroke is a good thing for rowing, but for non-racers who don't row together often, a stroke that is too fast will be problematic. There must always be a recovery period between strokes while the boat continues moving forward. Or backward. If the recovery time is too short, the strokes will slow a boat by cutting off its glide. Too much physics? In Louisa's paradigm, the recovery time did not exist if the day was troubling. It was just *bam, bam, bam*! Keeping up with her, much less rowing in tandem, was a pure pipe dream.

On race day, Louisa shouted an Italian saying comparable to "bring it on" in English, although it translates into "ass of the whale." Go figure that idiom out!

Louisa had NOT had a satisfying week at work and was taking it out on the water. Her stroke was so fast that no one could sync with her. There was much frantic splashing, and they finished the race waterlogged. They came in last but were heard to shout "ass of the whale" as they crossed the finish line. This is how rec rowers race. For fun. Definitely not for glory.

The Panthers, except for me, had daytime jobs. We wore running and bike shorts instead of made-for-rowing-with-cute-little-logos clothes favored by the more fashionable crews. We didn't worry about covering up the spandex shorts since we never had the energy to go out at the end of an after-work row. We carried extra socks, water bottles, and headbands or baseball caps in whatever leftover canvas bag survived in the back of our closet from some long-forgotten convention.

Our tops were generally old cotton T-shirts and T.J. Maxx, five for $3.00 a bundle of white socks, so when one disappeared into the lint tray in the dryer, an entire pair was not bust. Water bottles were old, dented metal affairs that got refilled for each row with tap, not bottled water. Shoes were the Walmart-variety flip flops for $1.99, often in gross, neon colors or dead black, whatever was on sale.

When we began rowing together, we were forty-four to sixty-three years old and subsequently became exceedingly adept at relieving the day's tension with humor and a gut-busting workout. We coined ourselves the Pink Panthers for no good reason other than I found four pink visors at Walmart one fine day. And the Panthers part just came along for the ride.

Our bow person, Lou, wears black oval toy spy sunglasses so she can see where we are going and what we are about to careen into. Since she developed a small skin cancer, she had taken great pains to leave no skin uncovered. Between the long-sleeved shirt, long pants, baseball hat, large round black spy glasses, and bandana, which she pulled up to above her nose, she closely resembled a Ninja warrior. As the rest of the crew would be moving the foot stretchers to where we were comfortable and arranging our "cookies," Lou would grab her oar locked nine-foot long port oar, one foot in the boat deck, the other planted on the dock, and strum the oar doing her best Roy Orbison imitation.

Lou shouts, "Are we going to have fun today?"

The rest of us crack up at her character, "You bet," shouts Ann. "Been a lousy day, going to be a great row."

Lou is always laughing, and her laughter would get everyone else going. Whenever she came down to the boathouse in the winter to join us for a workout on rowing machines, she brought her new favorite music on her iPod. She proceeded to cover the part of the rowing machine that tells you how well you are rowing with her hat because she didn't want to know her stroke rate or mileage. She'd strap her iPod to her arm, put in the earplugs, and the only thing we heard from her for the next forty-five minutes was her singing at full volume to whatever unrecognizable tune blasted in her ear.

She once arrived at the boathouse and announced that she was wearing her pajama bottoms since her rowing clothes were all in the laundry, and she had forgotten socks, so she was wearing roll-downs (knee highs rolled down to her ankles.) We all agreed she looked like Maxine, the old lady character on greeting cards with stringy hair hanging around her wrinkled face while holding a smoldering cigarette in a bony, claw hand and rasping such tips as "If you are feeling old just because your boobs are touching the hem of your skirt, lengthen your skirt."

Lou could be counted on to bring us the latest fads from her work cronies. The one about using testosterone pellet implants in their butts to stay aggressive at work kept us amused for a week. She seemed to have more than her share of river adventures as well. She was rowing a double, witnessed a car drive off the bridge into the river, and waited with the driver sitting on the roof until the help she had summoned showed up. In another row in her single, she came across a sinking boat with two college students already in the water and made them hang onto her boat as a floatation device till help arrived. She once stole into the men's locker room to fetch back the fan that they removed from the women's locker room, only to catch one of our more famous rowers in his skivvies and tell the entire club that he was a tighty-whitey man.

She is a dickens, with a glint in her eye and a laugh at the ready.

Down on the dock, as we engaged in the business of adjusting boat shoes, attaching oars, sliding into socks, stowing flip-flops on the dock, and tossing water bottles into the boat, the conversation would go something like this:

"Damn, one of those guys on the racing team must have tightened this shoe. I can't friggin' budge it," complains Ann. "Anyone have a woody?"

"Don't you sometimes wonder where the name 'woody' came from?" I ask.

"Look at it," Ann points out. "it's six inches long, straight, and rigid! What do you think?"

That garners a laugh from Lou.

"I don't think the guys should be allowed to use 'our' boat," states Linda emphatically. "Men should be rowing a heavyweight boat anyway. What's up with that?"

"Oh, the coach will let them take anything out in a pinch," croaks Ann. "They are so lame that it doesn't matter what they row." Ann, being on the club's board, knows all the latest gossip.

"Who the heck in that boat rows stroke?" I ask. "The shoes are all the way forward. Damn."

"I don't know; that's probably Jake. He's a lot taller than you are," Linda said.

"Let's buy our own boat," says Linda, always ready to work on a good idea. "I'm tired of all this adjusting."

We laugh at the absurdity of that suggestion at a mere $30,000.

"Yeah, wouldn't that be nice," says Lou dreamily.

"Hey Linda, how's your mom doing?" I ask.

Linda is one of those women who excels at being a nurturing mom. She should have had a houseful of kids but only had two girls and a job. She knows everyone worth knowing in Wilmington, Delaware. If she doesn't know someone, she finds and gets to know them. She is our source for all the latest gossip about, but not limited to, who is dating whom, what coach got fired, which boat ditched in the river and whose fault it was, who on the racing team is bickering and over what, what happened at the club's board meeting, and so on. Want to know what's happening? Call Linda. She is currently looking after her mom.

"Oh, thanks for asking. She needs a lot of attention now, so I'm running around trying to get her what she needs after work and coming here and then running home to fix dinner. I'm going crazy. I need this row," Linda shouts this last.

"Yeah, me too," said Ann. "The docs at work are being unusually obnoxious. It's either row or drink. Let's row!"

Ann worked at the local hospital doing IT training. She spent a lot of time with physicians who can be more than a little trying. She often showed up full of the day's anxieties and ready to blow it off on the river.

"Okay, let's work out all of our frustrations tonight, ladies," cries tiny Lou, our leader. "Shall we go up or downriver?"

"Let's row down to 'Up The Creek' and get a beer and a burger; I'm starved," I add, smelling French fries from a riverside restaurant.

Everyone chuckles, and Lou calls, "One foot in and down."

And we are on our way.

CHAPTER 10

My Story

It's time you learned a bit about me. I have three degrees. No, it's not because I'm smart, just fickle. My first degree in chemistry was for my mom. When she and I (she was Velcroed to her only child and controlled all decisions) interviewed with Sister Duck (I'm not making that name up) at the prospective Catholic college, the nun marveled at my high final exam score in chemistry (which most ninth graders failed that year) and suggested I might grow up to be a notable chemist.

I tried to explain to them that I hated chemistry and only did well on that year's chemistry exam because Bob was my lab partner. He was cute, an upperclassman, and didn't believe in homework. This was his second round in chemistry. I did all the lab work. He said he appreciated me. I swooned, inadvertently aced the final exam, and he failed it again.

My mother instantly got stars in her eyes at the prospect of her daughter, the chemist. No matter how valid my excuses for not becoming that chemist were, none assuaged her from her goal for her only daughter. I was doomed.

The second degree, an MBA, was for my employer. It did not increase my salary. But it did improve my confidence, and it was fun, although it was a lot of work in addition to a full-time job. It was here that I discovered my analytical ability. I had never studied calculus but had used it without knowing as I analyzed profits and expenses for programs I proposed at work. Having learned it first would have saved me a ton of time.

The third degree was in graphic design. I had initially wanted to study art in college, but we know what happened there. I hate to admit it, but Mom had a point. The chemistry degree did well for me in terms of my career. Much to my dismay, I discovered that I'm not all that great an artist, not even a decent graphic designer, and a complete washout at sculpture. How can anyone work on just one side of a piece of three-dimensional art and see how it fits with all the other sides you can't see unless you turn it around, giving you the same problem? Isn't this a little of what Picasso tried to solve during his Cubism period?

I also discovered in art school that I'm color-challenged. Not blind, mind you, but challenged. Intellectually, I know one can make any color by combining the three primaries. I spent hours studying the color wheel, sure that the "aha" moment of comprehension was just around the corner. Alas, it was not to be. I was astounded the first time I asked how to make flesh color, and the answer was something like two parts: red, one blue, one yellow, and one part something weird like burnt sienna. What is burnt sienna anyway, and how could you possibly get flesh color by adding blue to anything? It spoiled any dream I harbored of becoming a painter in my dotage.

Like my degrees, my career was a bit of a ramble. Making the best of my BS in chemistry, I began at a nuclear research center learning how to spell thallium, a radioactive isotope, and to operate a gas chromatograph. However, I can't remember why I did either. I found every conceivable way to contaminate myself with radioactivity, from not wearing gloves to pipetting (a glass straw thingy) by mouth. Yup, I swallowed it. When inevitably busted (from reading a dosimeter designed to detect my radiation exposure), I was marched to the contamination showers to scrub down with abrasive Comet cleanser, created initially to remove resistant stains from sinks and bathtubs.

I never told them I swallowed anything because I was terrified of what the remedy for that might be.

Acting in a few community theater productions, I was dazzled by the accolades, attention, and excitement. Dreams of becoming famous precipitated a move from radioisotopes to pursue my destiny as an actress, singer, and dancer. I had done some community theater and had even won a scholarship to a professional acting school in Buffalo, and it was time for the big step to summer stock where I could be discovered. I was about to receive a marriage proposal from a handsome wannabe actor who was then living on a friend's sofa in New York City, eating peanut butter and jelly sandwiches and tramping around the city from audition to audition. Visions of a husband and wife team, like Burton and Taylor, danced through my silly young head. Off I went to Indiana to make my name upon the stage.

They never tell you this when you audition for summer stock, but apprentices in professional theaters rarely get on stage. Mostly they build sets, locate props, change scenery, sell candy bars and cokes, usher, and, worst of all, clean the bathrooms. They let us do some children's theater, which was fun, and I had a couple of on-stage mini-parts in the equity productions, but nothing to help me on my road to stardom.

Nevertheless, by the end of the summer, all the young gay apprentices (I knew they were gay because after we would all go to our rooms, I would hear doors opening and closing to the musical chairs of bed-hopping, and my doorknob never turned) and I were infused with the smell of the greasepaint, the roar of the crowd, blah, blah, blah. None of us were discovered that summer.

Undaunted, I landed a job at the local professional theater back in Buffalo, where this fantasy all started as the assistant to the artistic director. It paid a salary, and although I never stepped onto the stage or observed a rehearsal, my boss put my name in every program as an understudy of one female actress or another. I suspect the latter was done to obviate having to pay someone a salary to assume that role.

I was whisked away from this far-from-lucrative paradise by the wannabe guy in New York who got tired of sleeping on sofas and had developed an allergy to PB&J. Someone needed to make a living. I landed a job in radiopharmaceutical research in Los Angeles, where he could make his move onto the big and little screen.

Like cats who avoid rooms with rocking chairs, the chemists I worked with avoided parties. The wannabe folks love them. People who choose this career path must become narcissists even if they don't present initially with that personality disorder. They worry constantly about where the next job will come from and know they must unrelentingly tend to their looks. It is not an easy profession, and even entertainers who make it are never sure of a steady income. They are all, of necessity, one-track conversationalists and, unsurprisingly, boring.

When one of the attendees spotted someone not of their wannabe tribe (me), they would politely ask what I did, not the least bit interested. But I might be a producer, director, screenwriter of something, anything. Someone who could get them the next audition, promote them for a part, a gig.

When I would tell them I was a radiopharmaceutical research chemist, their eyes either took on a patina-like polyurethane, or their faces registered disappointment that I was not the one to further their career. Some would buy a moment by sipping their drink and then excusing themselves to say hello to someone of interest. Or if they did hang around out of some long-ago learned polite behavior from their mother, they would tilt their heads as if they were genuinely interested, like a pooch tilting his head to understand if his human is saying anything about a treat or a walk or game, and ask me how dangerous nuclear power plants were. I worked at UCLA, where a small nuclear reactor provided our isotopes. I had no clue about the safety of a nuclear power plant. Actors hadn't a clue what nuclear anything was apart from dangerous, and my wannabe would further that illusion by telling them I glowed in the dark.

I did some showcase theater in Los Angeles. That's a theater that hires nonequity and Equity (card-carrying) actors. My wannabe was the assistant director of *Promises Promises*, an old musical. He insisted I come with him to rehearsals. Sitting in the front row next to the director, watching a rehearsal one night, the director turned to me, and asked, "Can you sing?" "Yes." "Can you dance?" "Yes." "Get on that stage. We need a bigger chorus."

My husband was polite about it, but his dream was to star in musicals despite his inability to carry a tune. I'm sure this move on my part rankled and was quite unkind of me. In retrospect, I try to blame it on Mom. This stage was much more fun than the chemistry, which wasn't. I wasn't discovered here either, but neither was the shy wannabe.

The misguided attempt to escape from chemistry to the infinitely more fun acting, singing, and dancing ended. It was okay because, as it turns out, I was not remarkable at any of those three things. Although he never quite got to be, the wannabe was much more talented than I. I did rub elbows with some who made it from summer stock. The set designer became the set designer for the Metropolitan Opera House in New York City, and one of the apprentices became a big star of a major soap opera on TV. Maybe if I had just persevered . . .

Five years later, the wannabe and I divorced. I didn't hate him like I hated chemistry, but I had visions of life with him being more fun. I pictured moments of joy and jubilation followed by others of sadness and pain, of dressing up and parties, dancing, and carousing. Alas, he was a normal human being despite the persona he projected. He often said I fell in love with the image. Must have.

The next ten years were a blur of career obsession and rotating partners. I could not stick with one guy for longer than a few dates. I wanted to be with someone but couldn't bring myself to be present enough to be vulnerable and trust—a leftover from my upbringing. I threw myself into my career, now as a department director for a chemistry nonprofit in Washington, DC. I finally got relief from arguing with chemistry directly.

At thirty-eight, having just finished a grueling executive MBA program and maintaining a 4.0 GPA while working full-time, I booked an extravagant vacation. Overseas Adventure Travel offered two weeks in Egypt on an adventure with only seven other people, all of whom were strangers. My companions were five women and one man. Most of the women were good travelers and around my age. The man was another story altogether.

He was forty-one and divorced. He was well-traveled and eager to share his adventures with everyone. He worked as a manager for DuPont in Wilmington, Delaware. I thought he was an arrogant geek. He later told me he thought I was a "doobner," but he could never explain to me what that meant. It sounded like a character Gilda Radner would play on *Saturday Night Live*.

After bonfires with the locals on the sands of the Nile drinking local booze and an overnight train trip to Cairo singing drinking songs with a group of Israelis in the bar car with the geek, I found myself warming up to him. I'm all in on vacation romances. Chances are that geographic locations guarantee you will never see each other again. None of the waiting for a phone call, email, or message from the guy you just met. What could be better?

It turns out Wilmington and Alexandria are only two hours apart. After three years of making phone calls, sending messages and emails, and spending weekends together, I talked him into getting married. The geek was not so geeky after all. It turns out life with him was always a party.

Bouncing around for a few months upon moving to Wilmington, I joined the second-largest medical professional association, the American College of Physicians in Philadelphia, as the director of the membership department. The CEO who hired me five years later had the audacity to leave, and the culture changed. I was not far behind him.

The University of Pennsylvania Health System needed someone to negotiate joint ventures with community hospitals. My job was to introduce community hospital administrations to Penn, which would be taking over many of their departments. It was like taking a bone from a dog, with lots of whining and fighting. I'm out.

I retired to study graphic design. I planned to get the degree and hang out my shingle. As it turned out, my husband was so jealous of all the fun I had going to school that he decided to retire too. His goal was to travel as often as possible, which is not conducive to starting a new career. It looked like I was now totally retired from any paying endeavor. Exploration of the myriad options for spending my days began.

CHAPTER 11

Kiss the Wall and Die

Is rowing the only worthwhile game in town? Heck no. There are myriad other options, and I've tried lots of them. I tried tennis only to discover I have no hand-eye coordination. I could serve like a champ, but when heading to lob a ball back across the net, I would shift my eyes to my racket, where I planned to hit the ball instead of the incoming ball. That pretty much shot the idea of another sport involving a ball. And for one reason or another, most of what I tried, either I didn't fancy or I sucked at.

My first whitewater rafting trip was on the Rio Generales in Costa Rica. I didn't know what to expect, but I have always believed nothing to be impossible, and this was just another adventure to be conquered. We were four with a guide to steer and call out moves in a small rubber raft. It was the first raft trip of the season, so the water was in full rush. It didn't take long for me to realize that the only place for a five foot four person to sit in this six-person raft was in the front. Sitting on a baffle with toes jammed up front in a crease, I could lean out the side to reach the water. Otherwise, I was air paddling and unable to respond to the guide's shouts to "paddle hard" in the middle of a rapid. The downside to being in front is you can't avoid seeing each calamity unfolding, like a big hole you're about to drop into where there should have been water!

We learned to high side to avoid spilling when navigating through boulders, to paddle hard enough to ride a wave just before the eddy coming out of a rapid called Chacalaca, to float the river if ditched with knees bent, feet in front of us facing away from the current and how to get back into the raft after swimming a rapid.

It was so scary that after we maneuvered through a rapid, I could smell the fear coming off the four of us: savory with a hint of garlic. Or was that from our lunch? But I had faith in our river guides and our young crew. So as we approached one of the rapids, the guide said the river would push us into a granite wall on the side, so you all must get to the right side before we hit the wall to keep the raft from flipping. Of course we were not quick enough on the "high side," and the raft flipped us all unceremoniously into the rushing river.

As I watched my feet and bent legs in front of me, I realized I was completely submerged and not breathing. A strange thing happened. A calm overcame me. I had no fear of drowning. The water was cool, clear, and quiet under the surface. I fluctuated between being amazed that I felt no need to breathe and wondering how far I would go before the current had enough of me and brought me to the surface. It did eventually gently spit me up. I was almost sad to leave its underwater majesty.

It was after the guides got us all back in the boat that they told us the name of the rapid, translated into English as "kiss the wall and die." To this day, I wonder what was going on in my brain while that river was having its way with me. I was peaceful enough to believe I could stay within its grasp for as long as it needed me there, that breathing was no longer compulsory.

Over the years, I rafted several rivers. Most came with incredible scenery. In Peru, the emerald green trees on the sides of the river provided a perfect pallet for the exotic birds of stunning reds, golds, and blues.

The most magnificent was rafting the Colorado through the Grand Canyon. We were a group of eight with three river guides and three rafts in that gorge for eleven days. When we weren't psyching out or maneuvering through the rapids, we were enchanted by the incredible striations along the cliffs, the amazing side canyons, the small feeder streams, the hikes back to waterfalls, the water etched-out caves. There was so very much to absorb to be almost wholly overwhelming. Like overdosing on the wonders of nature.

I had a wonderful trip in Chile, which included hiking along the Futaleufú River. We walked along the river, zip-lined over it, and were treated to one rapid. Being older and more apprehensive of ditching on this famously unrunnable river (meaning even the experts don't attempt to raft it), I craved the reassurance from our guide that the rapid we were planning to do was probably only a class IV (V is unrunnable), and no one ever ditched in it. Never say never. We did, of course, much to his amazement, go over. As we approached this narrow drop, I had a front-row seat and watched the river undulate in some unpredictable maneuver and then disappear beneath our raft, casting us headlong into the surf. The Futaleufú did me in. That was the end of my whitewater rafting days.

CHAPTER 12

Rockin' the Rockies

I took a weeklong backcountry horseback riding trip in the Canadian Rockies with Holiday on Horseback out of Banff, Alberta, every year for about seven years. The outfitter had permission from the provincial parks system to run these camping trips as long as he owned the company. He had been grandfathered in since the parks no longer allowed outfitters permits to take camping trips through the parks.

The trips were limited to seven guests with a cook, guide, packer, and a string of seven mules to carry tents, duffels, sleeping bags, and food. Each morning, we woke to cowboy coffee: throw grinds into the big kettle, add water, and put it on the fire; half an hour later, dump a cup of cold water into the pot to settle the grounds to the bottom, and voila. If you did happen to get a few grinds in your mouth, they just helped keep your teeth clean. The French Press coffee maker had nothing on cowboys.

Breakfast was an elaborate affair of eggs, bacon, toast, or pancakes over an open fire. They even jerry-rigged an oven to bake cakes and muffins. Lunch was a simple sandwich on a trail stop with the guide. Dinner was amazing. Large wooden boxes packed onto the mules contained fresh meats, vegetables, potatoes, and rice. These were quite the gourmet meals, especially appreciated out in the crisp mountain air. The last night, we were treated to steaks grilled on an open fire.

We always camped near rivers for water to cook, wash dishes, and clean the occasional body parts if you didn't mind the freezing snow-melt water. If you were friendly to the cook, they might let you warm some water to wash your hair. I was always nice to the cook.

I continued to go back to these trips year after year for several reasons. I have loved horses since Mom first perched me atop one at the age of two. It was a small pony, and before anyone knew it, he took off for the feed bag in the barn with me on his back. I stayed on him quite handily until he went under a horizontal barn board, where he unceremoniously knocked me off backward. I lay on the hay, giggling at finding a new best friend who liked playing with me. I was in love with the beasts. Later, I would learn that this was the first sign that between me and the horse, the horse's decisions ruled the day.

The horses on these backcountry trips were strong quarter horses able to manage any trail we might unexpectedly come upon. And large enough to intimidate most critters in the wilderness. They were sure-footed and safe in every regard. Knowing this, I could relax on their back, not even watch where we were going—a perfect situation for spending a week gazing stupidly at the glorious mountains from horseback. Also, we were not allowed to do anything more than walk. If anything happened to one of them on a trail trip, we would have no way to get them out. Trails festooned with tree roots or having to shortcut down a scree slope were hardly conducive to even a slow trot anyhow.

The first trip my husband and I went on was in September, and it was bloody cold. I don't think I washed my face for a week, to say nothing of other body parts. But the mountains in late fall hold a special magic. There is nothing to compare with riding along, listening to a bugling elk, and finally riding out of the forest to see the magnificent beast desperately calling for a mate. The mountains are always snow-covered on the peaks, but they are richly sparkling white everywhere in September. There are even areas of blue and sometimes pink snow from algae. And while the air is always fresh and clean, it has an extra crispness in the fall.

That was the trip where my husband, Paul, decided to dry out his favorite Frye leather boots by hanging them over the fire. By morning, they had shrunk, and he couldn't get them over his size 13 feet. Those Fryes reside forever at the company lodge perched upside down on a couple of elk antlers over a fireplace. Wranglers and future guests enjoy a chuckle over the idiot guest who tried to dry out leather boots over a fire without stuffing them with socks, old T-shirts, or newspapers to prevent inevitable shrinking.

A nap after lunch was protocol, the three-hour ride supposedly wearing the city dudes out. On one of those occasions, we lay in a meadow at the tree line for an hour, watching a golden eagle soar and climb a thermal, simply enjoying his joy. On another, before dismounting, a group of gophers came to greet and rub noses with our horses. They did not fear us or the horses and gave in to their curiosity. Truly magical.

There were grizzly sightings every trip, mostly from afar, but close enough to see what they were up to. One afternoon, we suddenly came upon a mother and her two cubs, but the guide rerouted us before she could see us. The guides regaled us with the story of a ranger, new to the job, who found a half-eaten moose carcass and decided to use it as a seat while he made note of it in his ranger book. Of course, the bear returned to claim his supper, and the ranger was forced to climb a tree. The bear followed him up the tree, and the ranger spent the next hour leaping from one tree to another to keep away from the bear and frantically using his sat phone to call for help.

Another ranger had been told it was an excellent idea to let bears know you were around so as not to startle them. Many hikers use bear bells for this or shout yahoo every quarter mile. But this one alerted his presence by woofing, not the sound a dog makes but the deeper sound bears make to warn intruders to *vamonos*. This ranger walked right into a bear's path, woofing. Another ranger up a tree. Bears two, rangers 0.

One of the guides was exceptionally handsome and radiated that macho, rough-and-tumble, horse-whisperer vibe Hollywood drilled into us when we were young, impressionable girls. In these movies, the tough exterior hid a kind, gentle soul inside (think Gregory Peck in *High Noon*). Real cowboys spend their lives in barns, bunkhouses, and outhouses, getting bucked off bulls and horses and sleeping outside in a bag on the ground. Whatever gentleness, kindness, or warmth they might have in their souls is reserved for the nonhuman four-legged species they spend their days with. They are skinny, calloused, and wiry. This guy filled in all the boxes for a cowboy, except he was so incredibly handsome you ached for him to epitomize the Hollywood version. But regardless of what was hiding at the bottom of his soul, when Mr. Handsome Cowboy removed his Stetson, the poor guy was badly balding. It stole his appeal like a plump person removing their Spanx.

At our insistence, our guide relayed a story the wranglers voted among the top ten. A packer was trying to pack guests' duffel bags on George, the mule. When the strap was cinched, George would buck, kick, and shake his head. The packer tried again, thinking George may just be having a feisty morning—same result. No matter how much sweet-talking the packer did, George was having none of this duffel on his back.

The packer gathered the guests, explained the situation, and asked whoever owned the offending duffel to see what might be inside that was making George disagreeable. As the guest was riffling through her bag, George whinnied. The packer knew instantly that whatever she had just touched was the offending item. "That's it, Mame," he shouted! The woman retrieved a gadget, which she apologized for leaving on automatic vibrate when pressed. Our guide finished the story by declaring, "What kind of woman brings a vibrator on a backcountry horse trip?"

I waited until the guests exhausted their good belly laugh.

"That would have been me. It wasn't a vibrator. it was a massager I bought at the airport for my husband's stenosis, which became aggravated after six hours on a horse."

I don't think anyone believed me. And even though I was laughing, the guests did an embarrassed quiet, and the guide got up to fetch the tequila bottle.

One of the trips moved from one pass to another every day. Each pass was higher and more magnificent than the last. And the way the trail wandered, we frequently didn't get a glance at the next pass until we were rounding a corner. There are no words to describe the emotional response to these majestic sights. Sometimes on a ride there would be no conversation. And sometimes I would catch someone and often myself looking and silently streaming tears. The Rockies are unforgiving and rugged and are no place for amateurs. Having been there, I now understand why humans throughout history have sought them out despite their hardships to get and be there. The world has many magical places, and I've been fortunate to see some of them, but nothing comes even close to the majesty of the Canadian Rockies.

CHAPTER 13

Horses Having
Their Way with Me

That love of horses kept me going back for more time and time again. I took English riding lessons in college and experimented with jumping until I went over the jump without the horse, even with the bar lying on the ground. Humiliating.

After retirement, I went back to try again. I rode four days a week this time and partially leased a horse. Friends joked that I must be leasing the front part of the horse because I had already married the horse's ass. In retrospect, I wonder, wasn't I the horse's ass to keep trying?

I'm told that some well-intentioned but clueless parents buy a horse for their kid and assume all the kid has to do is climb onto his back and say some magic word to get him going, and everyone knows all ponies stop when they hear "whoa." Many non-riders believe that learning to ride a horse is just like learning to ride a bike; a couple of turns around the block and a couple of spills and you've got it licked. Oh, that it was so. First, horses are very tall, and it's much farther to the ground than you think. Second, horses are alive and have their own minds, unlike most bikes I have known. Finally, horses are not equipped with handlebars.

Lastly, if you are riding English, there is nothing to hold onto when your horse picks up speed. If you use the reins to keep you upright, you pull the horse's head up or down, effectively making it impossible for her to see where she is going. This will also happen if you tug on the reins, begging her to stop. If you try to hold on with your legs, you're doomed. Squeezing her sides signals you want to go faster; thus it becomes even more challenging to maintain your rightful position on her back. As I watched five-year-olds ride around the ring bareback, I learned that the phrase, "It's so easy even a five-year-old can do it" does not imply adults have the same ability.

I lasted about three years as an equestrian determined to come to terms with my feisty Appaloosa, Betsy. She and I had different ideas of where to go, how fast to get there, and when to turn. After more than a few times ramming me into the rail around the ring, bucking at the flapping of a candy wrapper in the dirt, stopping dead in her tracks for no good reason that I could see, effectively bloodying my nose as I fell forward onto her neck, and blessing me with the slathers (horse throw up) as I tried to groom her. I gave it up. I got tired of Betsy having her way with me.

This disappointing fact of my ineptness was driven home at a dude ranch in Danby, Colorado. I thought I was safe there since all the horses were western. There was a horn on the saddle to hang onto and BIG stirrups to keep me steady. I did brave a *yippee ki-yay* gallop there, exhilarated and secretly terrified of embarrassing myself and breaking my head by falling off.

One afternoon I joined a class. Maybe this time, I would learn something to help me master this passion, at which I continued to fail miserably. There were three of us. We entered the rink individually and followed the instructor's commands. "Mount your horse. No feet in stirrups. No reins." At least we were in a rink, so galloping into the sunset was not risky.

"Close your eyes. Now, walk your horse around the ring without using reins or legs." I watched two horsewomen, through a mystical communication between them and the horse, walk when she told them to and stop when she told them. I could see no physical movement from these women, and they didn't utter a word. According to the instructor, they just sat the horse to tell him to walk and moved that seat an undetectable bit to tell him to stop. My turn came, and I just sat there. I had no idea what to do. My horse didn't either. We failed the course in spades. I proved to myself the undeniable fact that no matter how hard I tried and how much I loved horses, I was not destined to ride.

CHAPTER 14

The First Step Will Kill You

Next up? Technical rock climbing in the Canadian Rockies. No other living things could steal my agency in this endeavor. It, as I soon discovered, did have its ups and downs, pun intended.

"You want me to do what now?" My guide had instructed me to lean over the edge and pretend to sit in a nonexistent chair. This pretend chair hovered over a seven hundred foot drop. I honestly couldn't believe he thought I would do this. He assured me that I was harnessed, trussed, and tied into a rock and couldn't possibly careen to my death. It reminded me of the guide on the Futaleufú River who promised rafts never go over in that rapid. Maybe I'd avoid death, but how about broken legs, arms, back, skull? As I argued with him about not believing I could do this, he unsympathetically told me to hurry up.

There is nothing that compares with the fear of that first insane step backward off the top of a cliff with nothing but a couple of carabiners and some twisted nylon rope to keep you from careening through the abyss to a crumpled heap at the bottom. And crazily, I did it again and again and again. The joy of realizing I would not fall after that earth-shattering first step was exhilarating enough to keep calling me back to the mountains. And the climbing up part, as long as I didn't look straight down, was great fun;

getting to the top was well worthy of an "attagirl." But then, there was that rappelling down again.

I cut my teeth on the Bugaboos in the Canadian Rockies, did some practice runs on the Shawgumps in New York state, followed with a mountaineering week at Adamants Lodge in Canada on glaciers, and topped it off with the Via Ferrata in the Italian Alps. The Via Ferrata, or Iron Way in the Dolomites, was created by the Italian army during World War I to aid in the movement of supplies and troops. It consists of tunnels, steel cables, pegs fixed to rock, carved steps, ladders, and bridges providing footings and handholds.

We traversed it using a climbing harness with two leashes attached. To avoid falling to certain death, you clip these short lengths of rope using carabiners onto iron cables or ladders affixed to the side of the mountain. When you come to an iron bar pounded into the rock to hold the cable to the rock every few feet, you remove one clip from the cable and clip it on the other side of the bar while still clipped on the first side with the other short rope. This is done with thousands of feet of empty air beneath you. Perfectly safe, right? It is until you came to a break in the cable where you have to unclip both short lines from any cable and move untethered as much as four feet finding your own hand and footholds And there is the question of the wisdom of using these bars and cables fixed one-hundred-plus years ago.

While getting ready to climb in Canada, I started weight training. I am good at this and have stuck with it. I explain to my friends that it keeps me healthy and vibrant and allows me to do most of what I want. But honestly, when you are an over-fifty woman, and your trainer is a mid-thirties male bodybuilder, you keep your appointments. And that doesn't even begin to describe the fun of working out with a gang of tattooed bikers.

There was a point when my trainer and the gym owner ganged up on me to encourage me to compete. They thought I could successfully challenge others in my age range. That range is an old lady. I was genuinely flattered.

However, there was no way I would don a string bikini, get on a stage, and pose for anyone!

After all this, climbing at the local rock wall and at a few places close to home was tame and didn't hold my attention long. And anyway, I didn't seem to be getting any better at this either.

CHAPTER 15

Rollin' on the River

Having dinner one evening at a seafood restaurant on the Christina River, my husband was distracted. He had trouble carrying on a conversation, so enthralled was he by a young, attractive blonde rollerblading along the river-walk. She looked beautiful, it looked fun, and I had to give it a go. I convinced my friend Gwen to teach me.

I fancied us gliding gracefully along the boardwalk, one long, easy push on my right blade followed by another long, slow push on my left, my tanned, taut body clad in a bikini, long blonde hair trailing out behind me, a Zen-like smile of contentment on my face, heads turning, sun shining. Oh well, you get the picture of the fantasy. However, once I bought the outfit to keep bones from being broken in a fall, I looked instead like the Michelin Tire Man.

Okay, so I figured a little protection to begin, but I would pick it up in no time. After all, I grew up roller skating. There was still hope for that boardwalk vision. What I didn't realize is that blading these days is different. It's faster than the old metal contraption I used to attach to my shoes with a skate key, and today's skates have only one roller instead of the training wheels we called skates with two rollers back in the day. What a surprise that was.

My performance was pitiful. It mainly consisted of putting on the brake every few seconds, bending over my knees to maintain balance and minimize the distance between the ground and my body, and hyperventilating in anticipation of the inevitable bone-shattering fall. I was so bad at this that I quit after four tries—the blading bag collected dust in the garage.

The water I had been staring at while grabbing onto the railings of the riverwalk to save my bones from being shattered by a fall started to haunt my days. It beckoned to me. Always on my mind like that infernal song you can't get out of your head. The pressure to be on it, not in it, was like a bottle of champagne getting ready to pop and take out a ceiling light. As a kid, I had a history of happy times in boats on the water. Some of the happiest, if I'm being honest.

We had a cottage on a lake while I was growing up, and my dad always had one boat or another, much to my mom's chagrin. He arrived home one Saturday with a big, hunky, black-and-white inboard named—appropriately enough given its color—the Eight Ball. Not having consulted with mom before bringing it home, he was behind the eight ball in more ways than one.

I loved that boat right up until the day it sank. You couldn't tootle around at a snail's pace or it would take on water, and it only had two speeds: slow and slower. One afternoon, it just burbled its way down to the bottom of the lake. Fortunately, Dad got the boat cheaply, for a song, or maybe even free. It was so worth the one season we had on the water, even if Dad and I had to bear the ire of Mom.

His next folly was a doozy. The company that made the boat must have been Rayson because everyone on the lake called it the Rayson Craft. There were many inboard boats on the small lake, but none could match the speed of the Rayson Craft. It became a legend. My dad was sooooo proud. He claimed the boat hit sixty miles per hour all out. It had no windshield, so those who enjoyed the full force of the wind, denying any possible conversation because their cheeks were puffed out like a wildly happy hound with his head out a car window, never questioned the claim.

We had so much fun taking strangers who had the misfortune to sit on their docks as we passed for rides and scaring them to death with the speed. My favorite move was to follow a slow-moving Cris Craft, which was creating a super wake. At top speed, the Rayson Craft could get airborne by jumping that wake. He forgot to tell Mom about this one until it showed up in the garage one day. He never quite grew up and was almost always—right along there with me—on Mom's shit list.

There is only a little traffic on the Christina, a tall ship, the occasional jet ski, and a couple of party boats. The river was not big enough for Cris Crafts, inboards that top out at sixty miles per hour, or water skiing, but it was perfect for rowers. So after all the searching for the ideal sport to keep me pumped, I landed in the cockpit of a shell. I couldn't hurtle to the ground and break anything, didn't have to see eye to eye with the boat to be successful, wasn't required to scare myself to death looking over an abyss every time I did it, and didn't have to worry about anything significant crashing into me. It looked like a winner.

And I got to be pretty good at it. Since I was over fifty when I discovered the sport, I was not interested in competing. Not only had I been the classic couch potato for the first forty years of my life, but I had logged some twenty-five years of heavy smoking, which took its toll on my aerobic ability. Rowing all out for six or seven minutes in a race was hell for me. I stuck instead to recreational rowing. This doesn't mean that I never raced, however. Recreational crews do compete, just not as vigilantly as racing crews.

CHAPTER 16

Adult Rowing Camp

I'm guessing that sculling camp is for adults, like summer camp for kids. We lower-middle-class kids went to the local park in the summer to ride bikes, play tag, and learn whatever crafts the town had cooked up for the park kids. It never occurred to my parents that they had to send me away somewhere for me to enjoy my summer. I can only assume that what I did in my second summer of rowing would qualify as camp.

Craftsbury Outdoor Center in Vermont is the first rowing camp for sculling in North America. It is a definitive training camp for scullers worldwide. Up to sixty youth and adult rowers can be accommodated in their week-long programs. Kids under twenty-six are called youth rowers, and those over that age are called masters rowers. Unlike other master designations like master craftsman, master gardener, or master chef, in the world of rowing, masters does not mean you have mastered the art of rowing. It does mean that you are no longer considered "youth."

It also means that when you race in a master's race, you compete with people from twenty-six to eighty-five. There are handicaps for older folks, which is really degrading; the word itself indicates that we older rowers are less competent. But these handicaps amount to just a handful of seconds, not enough to compensate for a thirty-year difference in body strength and endurance.

Accommodations at Craftsbury are spare. No massages, hot tubs, facials, or mani-pedi salons. Meals are no-frills cafeteria style and enjoyed communally on long tables with benches, sitting with people you don't know, using paper napkins. The food is decent and is always followed by a lovely, gooey, highly caloric dessert. After six hours of rowing a day, campers easily decimate huge ice cream drums long before they can melt. In the evenings, there is no TV, phones, or Wi-Fi. There are workshops, not on survival skills or craft-making, but yoga, off-season strength training, using the erg, and the tedious physics of rowing.

Four of us from our boathouse decided to venture to the crème de la crème of sculling camps. At the time, only one of us knew how to scull; the rest, having only learned to sweep row, would be starting from scratch, learning to scull in a single. We knew each other only from a casual row or two. Sarah began letting it be known around the boathouse that she was going on a particular date, and one by one, three more of us decided to tag along.

We were Ava, Sarah, Gwen, and me, all fifty-something athletes. Ava was our entertainment, Sarah our competition junkie, and Gwen, our beauty queen. I rounded us out with some humor and a penchant for noticing and lusting (only in my heart) after good-looking, fit young coaches.

When viewed from the top, a single scull looks a lot like a twenty-six-foot by eighteen-inch brightly colored fish with nine-foot fins reaching straight out into the sea. It's long, skinny, shiny, and pointed at both ends. It is unwieldy if you don't know how to handle it in or out of the water. There is no rudder or keel, bottoms are round as with all rowing shells, and there are no other crew members to help keep the balance or blame if things don't go well.

When a single scull is carried upside down on your head, you swear it's the length of a tractor-trailer. Finding the balance point is a challenge, particularly for newbies. If you miss the midpoint, you engage in something that looks suspiciously like those 1960s plastic toy birds people decorated their car dashboards with that bent forward bobbing to drink and then popped back upright again, which, once started, would seemingly go on forever.

The scull's bow often nods toward the ground; you jerk one hand slightly forward to correct that. Then the stern goes down, threatening to hit the dirt, and you have to hop the other hand backward a bit, all the while supporting the thirty pounds of the boat on your head. When the bow dips again, you pull the stern hand back just a little, and so on. Like with the plastic birds, once the dipping cycle has begun, the only way to stop it is to put the boat down and start over again. At camp, the ramp to the water was filled with a sea of bobbing plastic birds.

Lesson one at camp was about getting back into the scull after falling out. The coaches did not even argue with us about whether we would fall out. They assumed that a time would come when, no matter how many yoga classes we had taken, each one of us would find ourselves off balance enough to result in a swim. They were determined to teach us how to recover from the inevitable.

For some reason, this exercise scares novice scullers. Ava had been rowing single for ten years, so she would laugh and say, "Hey, tootsies, it's a piece of cake. The only thing to be afraid of is not being able to turn the thing over and drag your sorry ass back into the boat. Now that's embarrassing."

That's not exactly encouraging, Ava. As we got closer and closer to the dock and our time to "ditch," we made more inane attempts at nervous humor. "At least we get to practice in clean water. Imagine trying to do this in the cancerous Christina," joked Sarah.

"I think I have a sudden case of PMS and need to go to my room," I added.

"It's not going to work, honey. Your hot flashes tell us that you are post-menopausal, and we'll tell on you," Ava chortled.

Ava had sculled for ten years. Her physical presentation was all athlete. She wore her blonde hair cut very short and spiky and was a thin, flat-chested woman who appeared to be just a tiny bit bow-legged, which, in addition to her hair, lent a butchiness to her appearance. She had tons of energy, found humor in absolutely everything, and laughed after everything she said. We all laughed with her because she was funny, creative, playful, and unassuming.

Sarah said, "If we can row sweep, we certainly have the strength to pull ourselves out of the water into that scull."

"Of course, we are older than most rowers here," Gwen quietly commented.

"Yes, but we are women, and women have the power to do whatever is necessary," I reassured, "unless, of course, we develop a case of hives. I think I'm starting to itch."

"Not going to work, Danielle. If you want supper, you must swim," reasoned Sarah.

"I could go without supper." I had an angle for everything.

"What's the worst that can happen? If we can't get back in, the young hunks swimming around to help will have to shove our sorry asses into the scull. Can't say that I would mind my bottom being shoved into a scull by him," Ava laughed, nodding toward the coach in the water.

"Hmmm, but I really can't do this. I just had my hair permed, and you know what they say about not getting it wet for twenty-four hours."

With that, Ava grabbed my arm and began the march to the front of the line. "Come on. No excuses. We are all going to make asses of ourselves together."

"No," I complained, followed by a very audible sigh, "Ohhhh, nuts. I really don't want to do this."

As with the squeaky wheel getting oiled, the biggest chicken gets to go first. Shoved to the front of the line, I was helped from the dock into a single scull for the first time. I'm sure my helper was cute, but I have to say I didn't notice, so terrifying was the prospect of the immediate future.

"I don't like going under," I explained to the coach in the water, helping me move the boat away from the dock, "I always get water up my nose. This is my first time in a single," I further qualified. "I'm not exactly comfortable,"

I admitted with a laugh. "And I'll give you $50 if you tell them all you know I can do this and let me go without the trial," I tried.

He laughed. "That's the best offer I've had today. Don't worry, I'm right here."

"Okay," he said as we got far enough from the dock to commence with the exercise. "When I tell you to, you are going to pull your left arm back so that your oar is parallel to the boat, keep your right arm centered in the boat with your right oar perpendicular. The boat will automatically and slowly tilt left, and you will fall out. As you fall into the water, try not to let the oar handles hit you on the head."

"I don't want to do this. I don't want to go under the water."

"You don't have to. The turn will be slow, and you can just fall into the water and keep your head above. There is nothing to be afraid of; I will be right here."

"Yeah, easy for you to say."

"Okay, let's go now."

With that, I pulled my left arm back, kept the right one in front of me, and felt the boat slowly tilting me into the water. "Oh, shit," I muttered, "here we go."

"Don't worry, I'm right here."

I was in, and the good news was that I hadn't gone under. The bad news was that there were oars everywhere, floating toward my head and tangling in my arms. And the boat was huge. It looked enormous upside down in the water and very unmanageable.

Out of breath and sputtering, I yelled to him, "Now what?"

"Calm down and grab onto the boat for flotation. The boat won't sink, so you can hang on and catch your breath."

I put one hand on its slick surface and slid right off. "Got another idea?" I asked.

He laughed, "Grab the oar handle; they float too."

I did as I was told and relaxed. After all, I was only ten feet from the dock here. But I was soon too anxious to wait any longer. "Now what do I do?"

"First, reach over the hull and pull the oar on the other side of the boat parallel to the boat."

"You've got to be kidding me." But I managed with a foot flutter and a grunt to reach over and place that oar where he wanted it.

"Okay, now do the same thing with the oar on this side and turn the boat over."

"How many arms do you think I have?" I shouted at him as I struggled to tread water, continue breathing, and perform the complicated maneuvers he bid me to do.

Much to my surprise, the boat flopped over, as he knew it would, and I calmed down a bit.

"Now you will reach over and arrange the oar on the other side of the boat to be perpendicular to the boat, then do the same with the one on this side. And when they are both perpendicular, you will hoist yourself up onto the seat."

"Ha, what have you been smoking?" I laughed. "How the hell do you expect me to do all that at once?" I worked to get the oars into position.

"Okay, big kick in the water and pull yourself up. When you are up, twist and sit on the seat. It's just like getting out of the water onto a dock. You've done it a thousand times before."

With that, I kicked like hell and pulled, then pushed up, hefting what felt like a three-hundred-pound body into the boat. I twisted and landed, sitting exactly where I was supposed to. Proud of myself, I smiled at my success and promptly slid back into the water.

My assistant laughed and declared, "That was pretty funny, but you forgot to put your feet into the boat."

"And you forgot to tell me that part, buddy."

"Sorry, I thought it was intuitive."

The laughter from the dock hardly penetrated my psyche. And I could no longer hear what my water coach was saying. This had become a war. I was going to get this if my life depended upon it.

I was mad. I arranged the oars, overturned the boat, and blocked out all other input. This was between me and this skinny, slippery boat. I had it. All I had to do was swing my legs into the boat after I was up and grab the oars. I could do this.

Okay, here we go. Kick, pull, push, twist, flop, swing up and in, grab oars, and I was sitting upright, ready to row—well, lah-de-dah. I acknowledged the applause from all the dock people and the treading coach. I grinned from ear to ear and patted the side of my boat, now my friend. I also knew, without a doubt, that no matter where I ditched this scull, I could get myself safely back into it. But I guess that's what this lesson was all about.

Ava managed to get into the boat on her turn the first time she tried, but she had been through this before. Sarah and Gwen both got in but took a couple of attempts, which were less dramatic than mine. All in all, we came away initiated. All the fear and anxiety of being there at all had evaporated. We were ready for whatever the week had to offer.

CHAPTER 17

Camp Follies

After a couple of days, I was, not surprisingly, crooning over one of the coaches like a cougar over her kits (pun intended). He was thirty-five-ish, cute, taught yoga, was blond, sun-dappled, and had a great body—well, you get the picture. And since it's no fun keeping these teenage longings to yourself, all three rowing buds were heartily regaled.

One morning I found underneath my door a Xerox copy of an article about him winning the Nationals (a prestigious race). In Sharpie marker, it was written, "Hi Danielle, thought you might enjoy reading about my glory moment." And it was signed "George," my cute, young kid. I figured he had put this underneath everyone's doorstep.

When I got to breakfast, I showed the copy around and asked if everyone got one. My three friends said no, they had not. I asked some others at breakfast, and they said they had not gotten anything either. Now, I was genuinely puzzled. He hadn't shown any interest in me and was too young for me, but what would explain him singling me out?

Once on the water for the morning, I scanned the lake for him, wondering when I might catch a glimpse and flash a big smile. Oh, that was ridiculous. What the heck would he want with someone fifteen years his senior? Still, why would he single me out? Unfortunately, I had no opportunity to interact with him that morning to get any answers. The mystery had me, well, mystified.

Maybe he was shy. Perhaps it was up to me at this point. I contemplated assuming the role of Kathleen Turner in *Body Heat*. But I knew I was in Turner's league only in some other life, and he wasn't William Hurt either. He was soooo cute. And this was soooo silly.

The girls asked me if I had seen him and if he had said anything. I answered no but that I would engage him in conversation about the article after the afternoon row. I wasn't sure what to say, but I just had to know what he was thinking.

They started to laugh.

"I don't think that would be such a good idea," Ava laughed.

It was Ava's practical joke. And she had gotten me. She was good. She had found the article, written the note, showed it to the others, and slipped it under my door that morning. And everyone else had played their roles well enough to win parts in a Broadway revival of Chicago.

Our schedule was grueling for something voluntary. Up at 6:30, on the water by 7:00 for a two-hour lesson and practice, breakfast at 9:00, back on the water for another two-hour lesson by 11:00, lunch at 1:00, break for workshops in the afternoon, then back on the water at 4:00 for another two hours and dinner at 7:00. Whew.

We were learning all about holding our oars with the lightest of touches as if they were tiny birds we could crush in our fists. They taught us to think of pulling open a bag of potato chips on our lay back. We were told to relax our shoulders and push with our legs, thinking of our fingers as eagle talons dragging back on the oar handles, exerting pressure neither up nor down.

We were mainly inundated with information and just trying to stay afloat on these slippery, razor-thin rockets. Rowing one of these babies felt as nerve-wracking as trying to walk a straight line when the cops stopped you for a DUI. Only in the case of sculling, instead of using our arms to keep our balance, you had to manage nine-foot oars.

My major faux pas of the week occurred on day two. In passing Sarah, I happily allowed myself to twist and look at her to make some favorable comments about her technique—silly me.

At this moment, in my obliviousness, I naturally pulled one oar parallel to the boat as my body turned to say hello to her. As predicted in our first lesson, I slowly toppled. No worries, I knew how to get back into the boat with aplomb, but Sarah kept rowing. I may have caught a slight upturn at the corners of her mouth as I began to ditch, but she did not stop, ask if I was okay, take a second look back, or even uproariously laugh as Ava would have done. Could she be autistic, I wondered?

Her life was all about competing and winning no matter what she was doing. So driven was she to succeed that she aligned herself with those who share the competitive bug. Back at the club, after our camp experience, she would frequently walk right by me without so much as a hello. She joined the women's racing team and spent her time and effort palling around with them. I often wondered if she had no use for a rower who could not stay upright on the water.

That day I learned that the scull would not forgive the slightest infraction of Rule #2: Hold both oar handles at equal height with blades flat on the water when not rowing.

These boats are multitalented and can teeter-totter on the water too. In this case, a tilting movement can be achieved by lifting one oar handle and lowering the other simultaneously. Of course, if a novice tries this on the water, the boat usually goes over. Rule #3: Hold both handles at equal heights when rowing.

Another sure way to ditch is to violate Rule #1: Never let go of either oar.

They taught us not to pull up on the oars as we did when we were kids rowing rowboats on summer vacation but to use the eagle talons to pull the handle straight back, blades just barely under the surface.

And lastly, Rule # 4: Don't ever pull either oar through the oarlock into the boat. I discovered the validity of this rule that first season back on our river. I got too close to a barge and pulled my oar in to avoid hitting it. As sweet as the first time in Vermont, my single did a nice slow rollover and deposited me in the water.

Not only were we inundated with information and fear of breaking the rules, but we were rowing six hours a day. No one rows six hours a day except the Sarahs of the world.

After three days of this grueling schedule, Ava decided to skip one of our two-hour daily rows. I was more than happy to play hooky with her. We drove into town to poke around. Ava declared since we all had to row in a race on the last day, we should do it with style.

We located all the mom-and-pop general stores where wooden floorboards creaked, groaned beneath us, and smelled like old wood. We roamed from aisle to aisle, inspecting the offerings. She would pick up some unknown thing wrapped in plastic and blow the dust off to see what it was. "Hey, these artificial pink flowers are cool. I bet we could use them somehow," she'd laugh. Into the basket I carried to hold our treasures, they would go.

And we were off to an unlikely five and dime where she found pink stretchy headbands. "Okay, this will work great. Now we need some bling." And we proceeded to look for anything that glittered. It was a potluck in these small village stores, left over from some earlier time before the Kmart moved in. But that didn't deter Ava. She just got more creative.

I had no idea what she was up to, but I kept plopping her chosen goodies into my little basket. Glue was next, needle and thread, glitter and stick-on stars. We went back to camp with our bagful of rejects from an earlier age, and she proceeded to glue and stitch these gorgeous flowered headbands for the four of us.

She presented these beauties to Sarah and Gwen, who thought they were terrific. Ava laughed her friendly we're-all-in-on-this-together laugh. On race day, we proudly announced that we were the team from Wilmington Rowing Center and wanted to be remembered for something other than our race times, which were sure to be abysmal.

On day six, our last morning, all sixty of us participated in a race from one end of the lake to the other. We were timed, so we didn't have to go neck and neck down the course. It's good since some of us were new at this and not so good at steering. These sculls are fragile, and bumper boats would not be a smart game.

We all took off in small groups at different times, with the predicted slower groups going last to minimize congestion. Being in the slowest group was a little disappointing, but at least I felt less pressure from expectations of doing well against the younger and experienced rowers. Since I didn't know what I was doing and felt a little unsteady, I played it safe and went slow. Well, I didn't exactly plan to go slow. It kind of just turned out that way.

Gwen finished next to last, but with her long, gray mane picking up the sunshine and her beautiful face framed with her pink flowery headband, it mattered not a hoot. Not surprisingly, I came in dead last. Sarah came in ahead of all the novice racers, and our experienced Ava was in the top twenty.

What was fun about that race was that by wearing our pink flowered headbands, we revived the 1950s glory days when Ester Williams, the sexy swimmer of motion picture fame, created a fashion statement and a successful movie career out of fancy bathing caps. We rocked even if we didn't know what we were doing.

Upon returning to our boathouse full of myself and high on whatever single sculling technique I had mastered, I ordered a boat and oars. I reasoned that I would have my trusty single if I ever got stuck without a quad. I took more than a few embarrassing spills in that nasty river, but I could always get back up and row home. My boat was a BMW electric blue. It shined like a sleek, colorful parrot fish, which I banged and scraped the bloody hell out of doing every one of those things not recommended to do in a fragile single.

CHAPTER 18

Parts, Pieces, and Purposes

Let's commence with the insufferable chore of learning the basics. I have to do it for you someplace; here is as good a place as any. Think of a zucchini cut in half lengthwise and hollowed out, and you have the shape of a sweep and sculling boat.

The Configuration

There are nine participants in an eight: eight rowers sit in a single file, and a small person (coxswain, or "cox" for short) faces the rowers and the boat's direction. Her job is to get rowers safely to and from the dock and steer the boat on the water. Rowers learn early on: you don't mess with, argue with, or ignore the coxswain—your life is in her hands. Coxswains rule!

Each person has either a port or starboard oar. The boat moves in the direction the cox is facing, and rowers are not. Who cleverly designed the sport to keep rowers oblivious to where they are going so they can concentrate on the power and speed? Or was there some other more nefarious reason?

The bow is in the front of the boat. Rowers face the stern, which should be the bow if they are moving in the direction they are facing. The stern is where the coxswain sits. From the perspective of the rowers, the port is on the right, and the starboard is on the left. If they were facing the direction of the boat, it would be reversed. It's only a problem when rowers jump into any other boat on the planet and try to reorient their brains.

Each rower has a hard plastic or wooden (uncomfortable) seat fitted with four small wheels on the bottom (one on the right and left in front and one on the right and left in the back). These wheels on the seat bottom slide along two metal rails, about a yard long, fixed to the boat's deck. The space between these two rails is where rowers step in the boat without breaking through the hull, incurring a debt large enough to warrant a second mortgage. All other spots are "no step" zones.

In front of each rower is a metal bar jutting out from the gunnels (the sides of the boat used to help get in and out of the boat and carry it), parallel to the water. These metal bars are called riggers, referred to when a coxswain yells "watch the riggers." They are rigid, solid, metal protuberances that will jerk a boat around if one hits a doorway, person, or immobile object while the boat is carried to, from, or on the water. They are a precision part supporting the oars and affecting the physics of the stroke, which we will not discuss here or anywhere else. It needs to be more exciting and necessary for rec rowers to fret over. Just know they are not to be used to carry the boat and need to be protected from banging into objects or people.

The port rowers have a rigger sticking out toward the right, and starboard rowers have the left at about a thirty-degree angle to the gunnel and parallel to the water. An oarlock is attached to the end of the rigger, reaching out three feet over the water. That is where the oar goes and is locked down. Duh!

So as not to make it too simple, the oars can be locked into the oarlock backward. When rowers begin a new season, this is not an uncommon error. The boat is un-rowable when this happens, alerting the rower that he has made a very silly mistake, and back to dockside they go.

We did have a single sculler who ditched with alarming frequency, and the safety officer questioned him to figure out why. Turns out the rower was not locking the oarlock. His oar would fly up and out of the oarlock, and over he would go. He was convinced he was often swimming because of an equipment malfunction. Even an ER doc can screw up.

Oarlocks adjust a rower's stroke length, height, and comfort using cookies, which are plastic circles that snap onto and fit around the post of the oarlock. These little yellow thingamabobs are designed to raise or lower the oar in the oarlock. There are usually four at each oarlock, and people fuss around arranging them over or under the oarlock.

"Did I use two on the top and two on the bottom last time?"

"I thought you tried three on the bottom and one on top."

"Were there three on the bottom on port and two on starboard, or did I try both the same?"

"Did I like rowing with them that way? I can't remember?"

They get adjusted so often that rowers will forget where they had them set. In fairness to rowers' short-term memories, each boat will require the cookie adjustment to be a little different.

The nine-foot oars are fitted with collars. This is not a fashion statement but a way to keep the oar from sliding through the oarlock. Part of that oar needs to be inside the boat for the rower to use it, so it needs a ring fixed around it to keep it from totally falling through the oarlock. Trust me, it's necessary, and it works just fine, even if you can't picture it.

Each rower has one port or starboard oar, and the blades (wide parts at the water end of the oar) are not shaped the same, so they must choose the right one. Often, these are color-coded just in case people forget what blade-shaped oar to use. The red or green bands on the oars distinguishing port from starboard oars are an embarrassment saver, particularly for novice rowers.

Then there are the shoes. Shoes are in front of each rower. They are fixed to a metal plate, slanted toes to stern, heels to bow, at about thirty degrees. These provide a platform for rowers to push against at the drive part of the stroke, where power counts. These shoes are fixed in three places with wingnuts and are moved almost every row to accommodate differing leg lengths. Sometimes they have been tightened so hard that you use a gizmo called a woody (made of, you guessed it, wood) to loosen them. You can't buy these in a store. Some fairy godmother (or father) in our boathouse makes them and leaves them lying around.

Rowing Positions

Positions in a sweep (and scull) boat are numbered from the bow. The seat closest to the coxswain is the stroke, seat eight. The seat behind her is seven-seat, followed by six, five, four, three, two, one (aka as bow). Seats seven and eight are considered the stroke pair, one rows port the other starboard. It then repeats down the line, alternating port and starboard. Seats bow through six follow precisely what the stroke pair does.

A sweep boat's middle four rowers are the powerhouses, the front two stroke setters, and the bow two steerers. Small people are generally elected to row in the bow as the boat narrows considerably at that end. People with good technique who can hold a stroke rate consistently are in the stroke seats. The guys in the middle do all the heavy lifting.

Stroke rowers are often full of themselves, heady with the power of having everyone follow them precisely. Bow rowers set the direction, maneuver the boat out of tight spaces, and sometimes balance the boat while others row. The middle guys have their heads in the clouds, knowing the boat goes nowhere without their power. They are the hulks.

Sweep boats come in eight, four, and two (referring to the number of rowers required). Their shorthand designations are 8+, 4+, 2+, or an eight, a four, and a pair. Some sweep 4+ have a coxswain, some don't, and a pair never has a cox.

Sweep versus Scull

The difference between sweep and sculling is that sweep rowers use one oar per rower, and scullers use two. Scullers row backward just like sweep rowers. Most rowers learn to row in a sweep boat, and many graduate to sculling over time.

Sculls come in eight, four, two, one. Their nomenclature is octopod, quad, double and single, and abbreviations are 8x, 4x, 2x, 1x. Sculls generally don't have coxswains. The bow seat is in charge.

Dissection of a Stroke

A stroke is the time from when the oars are initially dropped into the water until they are in position to drop in again. When you begin the stroke, your arms hold your oar handle as far forward as your body will allow, thighs pressing against your torso. This is the point at which the oars are dropped into the water, the catch. The goal is to have everyone drop into that water at the same time as the stroke rowers do.

Rowers then push as hard as they can against those shoes using thigh and butt muscles, and when their legs are straight, they lean back and pull their arms back till the oar handle is close to their body. This portion of the stroke is called the drive. The drive should be quick and hard.

The end of the drive happens when the stroke rower pulls their oar out of the water. At that time, the blades at the end of the oars are feathered. That means the oar is turned with their hands so that the oar blades lay parallel to and above the water no more than a few inches.

At this point, rowers use abdominals, quads, and glutes to slide the seat up to the starting position slowly; this recovery should be done slower than the drive. The boat glides while the rowers move up to the catch. To do the recovery too quickly will interrupt that glide and slow the boat. Sounds counterintuitive, I know. It's part of that physics stuff we don't want to mess with.

Upon reaching the catch's starting point, the oars must be feathered again so that the blades will be perpendicular to the water for the catch. Blades are dropped into the water by raising the hands at the catch. And another stroke begins.

"Skying" means someone in the boat is flying their oar too high above the water on the recovery. "Digging" means someone is rowing with their blade too far down in the water. Digging is normal for novices whose rowing experience is probably the old rowboat style. But either of these will disturb the set or balance of the boat. If a boat's balanced, it is not down on port or starboard, but rather perfectly balanced side to side on the water.

Commands

When a coxswain says to "hold water," all rowers rotate the blades to be perpendicular and drop them into the water, keeping them steady to stop the boat as quickly as possible. This command causes rowers anxiety. It's usually shouted and is the order to prevent a collision.

"Waynuf" is another command that requires rowers to stop rowing or walking while carrying a boat. Often, this call on land is to avoid hitting some idiot in the boat's path. Rowers can be remarkably oblivious when hanging around the boathouse yakking. Another call is reserved to alert these numbskulls that a boat is coming their way and they are in danger of bodily harm. This call is "heads-up" and is frequently ignored by the idiot numbskulls.

"Hard starboard" and "hard port" are terms used in the boat to indicate the boat's course needs to be adjusted. If hard port is called, rowers on the port side (right) push harder with their legs on the drive, and those on the starboard side ease up a bit. In a scull, rowers push harder with their right legs and ease up with their left. These maneuvers are used to turn the boat. When the boat is back on course again, "row even" is called.

"Layhold" is a term used on land that means grabbing onto the gunnels in preparation for the next move. It may be followed by "overhead and up" (lifting the boat to carry it overhead) or "roll it" (swinging from overhead to place the boat on the water).

Once all adjustments are made to shoes and cookies and oars are secured in oarlocks, "one foot in and down" is the order for rowers to get into the boat.

Rowers are asked to "countdown when ready." Every seat beginning with the bow then shouts his seat number in order when he is finished fussing with shoes, seat, and cookies and is prepared to row.

Sit at the finish, and "row" is the command to begin the row.

When disembarking, the same "countdown when ready" is used to indicate rowers are ready to disembark. "One foot up and out" means putting one foot on the dock and lifting yourself out of the boat simultaneously. Getting into and out of the boat is done in unison to maintain the balance and to avoid having a boat drift away from the dock without a full complement of rowers. A sweep eight can be rowed with six but not with a wayward two or three who couldn't get out of the boat with everyone else. No one gets out until everyone is ready to move.

CHAPTER 19

Single Sculling

I love my Panther quad, but single sculling is special. You don't have to talk to anyone; you can go wherever you want, stay out as long as you want, stop to admire that white heron if you like, listen to the birds serenade, wonder about things like where the many turtles sleep at night, relish in the smell of honeysuckle, and challenge yourself to be stealthy and quick enough to nudge the geese floating on the river with your bow.

It affords all the time you need to concentrate on the techniques you know need improving. I usually single out one thing each season to work on every time I row. With any luck, muscle memory will take over one day on that season's technique, and I can stop worrying about it and move on to the next challenge. If you choose one part of the stroke to work on per season, you can get to be a pretty damn good rower.

Going out in a single, you get to know the river better. The Christina has turns and bends aplenty. Each corner sends you into an area where the wind, which was buffeting your progress, may suddenly be at your back. The tide and wind combine to change the action on the water's surface. If the water looks too rough sometimes, you need to get around the corner from the boathouse, where the wind and the tide work together to create a calm reprieve. This also works in reverse, though. Suppose you are blissfully skimming along with what you believe to be a medal-worthy technique on calm water, and you round a corner where the wind and the tide are working in opposite directions. In that case, you face water rough enough to spoil your daydream.

Rough waters are challenging in a single. The boat is twenty-six feet long, and with that round bottom and no keel, it's a balancing nightmare. If you get caught in a situation where the wind has picked up quickly, you can try taking short strokes. There is a belief that short strokes will make it easier to balance in rough water. I'm not a fan. You're struggling to keep your oars above the water on the recovery and just below a roiling surface on the drive. Short or long strokes, the damage to the body is the same. The water bounces you around so that your shoulders, back, and arms are forced into a round of torture.

River traffic may create wakes that are just as bad as high winds. When this happens, it is sometimes best to stop and keep oars flat on the water as the boat rolls with the waves. These moments feel like when your car is out of control on the ice. You know you can't do much other than hold on and hope the gods are smiling that day.

One stretch of our river is where the shores are reinforced with concrete walls. This delightful area bounces any waves coming through back and forth for hours. Even the mild-mannered fishermen with their twenty-five-horse-power boats can get the waves a-rolling. We call this area "the bathtub." I'm not sure where that name came from. Maybe someone has a jacuzzi bathtub that makes waves.

Then there are the dreaded jet skis. It appears they are operated by kids who need to fulfill their daily bad behavior quotas. Or maybe the driver's wife was discovered cheating, or the boss just fired him, or he just totaled his car and needs to vent rage somewhere. Whatever prompts them, they seem to get a real kick out of bullying us. They circle us at high speed (do jet skis have a slow speed?) or rush back and forth, making those wonderful wobbly wakes for us to endure. We do think it worth reporting such lousy sportsmanship by getting registration numbers on these jet skis, but, well, we are too busy trying to keep the boat afloat.

Then there are those days when we get down to the river only to discover the water is sporting white caps or there is a storm brewing, and it's off to the coffee shop with the other thwarted single-rowing folks. We miss out on the row, but at least we catch up on the latest gossip.

Many people think singling is anti-social, but it doesn't have to be. There is a lot of time spent getting boats onto the water, back up, cleaned, and put away after a row. These elements of the rowing ritual require about as much attention as tying your shoes and as much time as you spend rowing. So it's a great time for conversation.

On our river, going out in a single can be dicey. In addition to the wakes you must contend with, there is a lot of debris on the Christina. Before you know it, you can find yourself halfway up on a log or debris field of limbs and leaves. Lily pads are growing on several shores, which entice and trap single rowers. Your equipment can betray you. You swim and cannot get back in because of equipment damage.

For these reasons and others, most singles rowers want a buddy on the water with them. Just in case of disaster. There's someone to chat with at the dock, in the boathouse, and on the river. Every singles row I've ever done with a buddy has also involved at least one conversation stop on the water. We might float halfway back on the tide, if lucky, without lowering an oar.

Some rowers, and I'm one, enjoy the solitude of single rowing. It's you and all the critters, trees, plants, water, air, and sun, accompanied by that repetitive, reassuring clunk of the oars feathering in the oarlock. The effect of that clunk on a quiet morning is as powerful as any chant I've ever heard muttered. Before long, I'm in that coveted Zen state.

CHAPTER 20

The Good, the Bad,
and the Downright Ugly

Like most other sports, rowing has a specific recommended costume. Unlike many other sports, however, it can be either delightful or disgusting, depending on the body it is adorning.

Baggy bottoms and long, loose shirts tend to get caught under the wheels of the sliding seat. Stretchy, clingy, short, breathable but not quite see-through spandex is the order of the day for bottoms. Upper bodies for women differ from men only with the addition of a sports bra, which unfortunately flattens boobs, a look neither attractive nor sexy.

Both sexes sport form-fitting racerback shirts designed to prevent chafing, or moisture-wicking unis (short bodysuits, often in the club's colors and logo), sweat bandanas, and visors equipped with dental-size mirrors to help them navigate their course de rigueur. Tops and visors are in jarring neon colors, begging to be seen by jet skiers, cigar boat enthusiasts, fishing skiffs, canoers, kayakers, and other river vehicles to avoid a surprise bash into a rower (or crew) moving at the speed of a tortoise, hardly aware of their course and often in an obliviously delicious Zen state.

When spandex was first introduced, stretch pants became the rage among women in the general population. Suddenly, we could breathe after meals, gain and lose those same five pounds without investing in new clothes, discard the fat-rearranging, jiggle-thwarting girdles without fear of hearing the remarks about their behinds resembling two badgers fighting under a blanket. Within a short time, females of all sizes and shapes enjoyed the unparalleled comfort of expandable waistbands. And after a few years, the scourge, "spandex is a privilege, not a right," was born.

Most female rowing shorts are worn mid-thigh and nicely cover any cheek peek exposures encountered with shorter shorts. The problem is that spandex, worn without underwear, which is the norm, is like wearing a second skin. The unfortunate occurs when one purchases a size too small or wears it after a few seasons when the body has morphed into a size larger. With its seam center front, the spandex short will bind the body a tad too tightly, creating a not-so-charming camel toe, leaving absolutely nothing to the imagination. This may not be evident in a bedroom dressing room but becomes illuminated in the bright outside sun. It is not an uncommon distraction.

When the bending, twisting, stretching, sprawling, and tangling into pretzels required of the rowing female during rigging is factored in, everyone pretty much knows more than you want about your body parts.

But this exposure thing is not all about women. As a privilege, not a right, spandex also works for men. It's even more in play with men since they have more to reveal.

There was a time when an email circulated a series of posed photos of different college crews. Crew members stood tall and proud abreast of one another, one hand proudly holding his collegiate oar upright, reminiscent of an Iditarod winner posed with his arm proudly caressing his lead dog. Photo after photo of these lean, good-looking young men with muscular, bared chests in black spandex, exposing substantial thigh muscles, graced my computer screen. These were often pleasant interludes to my workday.

Until "Ahhh!! What's that? Oh yuck."

A photo showed a crew wearing red instead of the standard black spandex shorts. It was a disaster. These remarkable athletes were proudly posing for their collegiate photo and blissfully unaware that they might as well have been posing naked. If an observer were not familiar with the male sexual anatomy, this photograph would serve quite adequate instruction. Every lump, wad, fold, dent, and wrinkle was evident in the shadows. There was nothing left for the imagination.

There was another photo of a regatta-winning team of eight men in *The Huffington Post*. The headline stated, "He Swore He Was Not Excited at the Time This Photo Was Taken." This could've fooled the viewer. And if he was being honest, then wow.

While researching a book on Rudolph Valentino, a 1920s silent film heartthrob, a friend of mine came across a promotional clip of Valentino as a member of a sweep crew. He was wearing the 1920s fabric version of spandex in light gray. It was not as tight as our spandex today; it was much less revealing but still suggestively shadowed. She was enthralled and hurriedly called to ask me if she might come to the boathouse and hang out. I emailed her the photo of the red collegiate team. Her ardor cooled.

Some male rowers indeed fancy themselves in spandex. These guys can be found after a row, standing tall, arms crossed, feet apart, hips jutted forward slightly, rocking back and forth on their heels, daring the females around to stare at their proudly displayed packages. They believe this is sexy. To you men, and you know who you are, it's not.

An all-gay club that races at many regattas wears the traditional uni in their club's colors, sporting the club's logo. But you don't need to see the logo to spot them wandering around before or after a race. It would appear fashionable for club members to pull the top of the uni down and parade around bare-chested when not in a boat. Hey, young men displaying nice chests. I'm not going to complain.

A few years ago, scholastic (high school) rowers decided that all rowing outfits, male and female, were gross. Most of them started wearing long, baggy shorts over their rowing spandex and whipping them off only at the last minute for fear someone would judge their not fully matured teenage anatomy. I can't imagine what they must have been thinking about the baby boomers' aging bodies grossly encased in spandex.

And lest I forget, there is another solution to the revealing spandex issue. Some manufacturers of rowing clothing have offered wildly colored patterned and striped spandex. You'd think that this would solve the problem, and it does. No more shadows, obvious wedgies and camel toes. However, women sporting this new look closely resemble beached whales, and men might be judged gay queens or just ridiculous. I've only seen two pairs in our boathouse, which was enough to keep the rest of us from investing our cash. Black continues to win the day despite its issues.

I need to add here that most rowers look damn good in their rowing garb. Rowing can burn eight hundred calories or more in each row, and many rowers are on the oars every day in the season. Do the math. We're talking 5,600 calories of goodies you can eat or drink weekly without gaining an ounce. Nice, huh?

CHAPTER 21

In Search of Boat Boys

Maturing women often discover rowing, which was once the fastest-growing sport among women over fifty. Most of these recruits are recreational rowers who have good reasons for their interest.

The muscles required in rowing are largely glutes, which are generally strong in women. It's a low-impact sport, so it's kind to aging joints. And, as I have grown to suspect, women have a specific gene for cooperation and compromise, positioning them favorably for success as members of any team sport.

Rowing is one of the few non–weight-bearing sports that exercises all the major muscle groups, including quads, biceps, triceps, lats, glutes, and abdominal muscles. It also improves cardiovascular endurance.

Except for the biceps, each of these major muscle groups are target areas for women. Marketers bombard us with the notion that taut thighs, high butts, and flat tummies are the only things that will make us attractive from the time we graduate from diapers into our first pair of pull-ups. And as we mature, such things as triceps, we are told, become important. No self-respecting female dares to do a sleeveless wave with sagging, untoned triceps whapping in the breeze.

Perhaps best of all, rowing burns more calories per hour than any other activity except cross-country skiing, allowing some of us to maintain bodies almost as skinny as the emaciated models we see in magazines and others to eat as many carbs as we want. There is no more perfect formula for a mature female athlete wishing to stay in the game into later years.

For a few seasons, I rowed in a quad with a crew of women, most of whom did not work for a living and could row at reasonable morning hours a couple of times a week. One of the crew members was Teri.

She had a perfectly proportioned body, was attractive and stylish, and was married to a talented businessman who draped her in diamonds, furs, and enchanting vacations. She was congenial, nonconfrontational, and easy to be with. Teri's signature attribute was her voice.

It didn't exactly make you squinch your shoulders and grimace as if you were listening to a truck scraping along the side of a Mercedes. And it's not as bad as the ear-splitting fire alarm screaming at you because the duck you are trying to roast in your oven is filling the kitchen with smoke. But take those two horrible sounds down a notch, add a Southern drawl, and you have it. It's not annoying, but in a crowded room, you would know she was there somewhere.

Teri was always coming up with new, novel ideas to solve all sorts of problems. I'm sure she must have fancied herself an engineer in a parallel universe. None of these ideas are in the least practical, although I'm not altogether sure she knows that. One idea she puzzled over all one summer was a way to get the boat down to the dock and back again without having to haul it ourselves.

"We need a hospital gurney affair that hydraulically adjusts up and down. It wouldn't be hard to make. I'll bet my husband could make one for us."

"The problem with that, Teri, is that we would still have to lift it over-head to get it into the water."

"Oh, yeah," she drawled, "I guess that would be a problem."

Or, on another day, "Maybe we could invent a pulley system to roll the boat onto the water upside right from the boathouse. Then we wouldn't have to lift it at all. And we could sell it to other clubs. Think of the money we would make."

"Well, we still would have to get the boat onto the pulley system, and how would we maneuver the incline at the water's edge?"

"Oh, yeahhhhhh," she said, "I forgot about that. But I'm sure there is some way to do this. I can't believe that some club hasn't figured this out."

"Most rowers don't mind carrying the boat to the water and wouldn't be caught dead with such a contraption," says Lauren, bringing us back from the fantasy.

Teri laughs but isn't convinced and is determined to devise a solution.

"I'm with you, Teri. You keep working on a plan," says Deb.

And then, one day, Teri's final suggestion hits a chord: "Okay, y'all, I have the solution. What we need are boat boys! We could hire some high school kids for the summer to meet us here, carry the boat down, meet us after we are done, and carry our boat back up to the house. We could pay them, what $10 a day?"

"High school boys? Yeah, that would work. Not," says Deb as we all laugh at the idea.

"The heck with teenagers," I pipe in. Let's find some forty-somethings to carry the boat for us."

"And insist they do this job in shorts with no shirts," twangs Teri.

"Roger that," says Deb.

"And, maybe they could even grease up a little so that their muscles would glisten in the sun," laughs Lauren, getting into it.

"Uh, where are we going to find these hunks?" I ask.

"We'll advertise in the *News Journal*. Boat boys needed, short hours, good benefits," says Teri.

Amid gales of laughter, "Do we have to spell out the benefits?" asks Lauren.

"We should be discrete, at least in the ad, until we get a look at them," Teri says.

"How about muscular legs, shoulders, and arms required," says Deb.

"Can we ask that they be good-looking, or would that be considered discriminatory," laughs Teri.

"Hey, maybe if we can find outstanding ones, we could publish a boat boys calendar with their pictures," says Deb.

Lauren says, "Oh, god, Mr. May, June, July. What a concept. Bet we could sell a bunch of those."

"I'll be the photographer," I croon.

"Oh, yeahhhhh," says Teri, "it's my idea and y'all get to have the fun."

"Let's talk about poses," someone offers as the conversation sinks deeper into depravity, and we haul our boat down to the water again.

One of our crew had knee surgery one year ago and eventually returned to the boat. But she brought her boyfriend along to help her carry and get into and out of the quad. Over time, he not only assisted with carrying and helping her into the boat but also took orders for coffee, handed crew their shoes when they came into the dock, and carried oars.

Finally, Teri got at least one boat boy.

CHAPTER 22

The Morning Quad

Rowing has developed a reputation as an elite sport for the wealthy. Everyone pays an annual membership fee and often a one-time bond when joining. If rowers gravitate to sculling, they might buy their boat and oars and spend thousands on a single scull. Then the rowing club will charge a storage fee and an insurance company a premium against damage.

If a recreational crew decides to enter a race for fun, there are trailering and entry fees. That same crew will probably opt for some coaching to not embarrass themselves with a poor showing, and they will also pay for that. It is a costly sport.

My first experience in a sculling quad was with the boat boy seeking morning group. These were experienced women rowers forty to sixty years old. Their kids are grown and out of the nest, some are married, some are single, some work, some work sometimes, some used to, some never did and don't ever intend to. These women are frequently spotted mid-morning after their row, sipping a latte together. They peruse the local sports shops for the most fashionable rowing togs between massage and pedicure appointments.

They share the latest yoga style discoveries, information about new trainers in town, where the best tennis courts can be found, the best golf clubs to buy, the biggest outdoor pools available, the latest diet craze, and the upcoming Fourth of July, golf, charity and social events that they will all attend.

"Hey, did you see those cute little skirts they were selling at Regatta last week?" Teri squeaks.

"Yeah," says Deb, "I bought one to put on over my rowing shorts for coffee when we go out afterward. It's adorable." Deb is a mild-mannered widow with three grown boys she raised. Her husband left her in good financial shape, so she does a lot of volunteer work. She's intelligent, sweet, thin, and has a thing for muffins, but only the tops, please.

"Nuts, I didn't see those," I say.

"You can get them online, I think. I'll get the brand name for you," says Deb.

And on another day . . .

"Hey, that's a great top; where did you find that?" asks Deb.

"There's a women's-only sports clothes place at the shore. I just loooooove the stuff they have there," drawls Teri.

And another day . . .

"Hey guys," says Lauren, "look at my new flip-flops. Aren't they adorable? Linda and I found them by Freddie's car wash at that little boutique. We each got a pair."

"They are soooooo cute," says Deb. "Did they have anything in green to match my rowing bag?"

Someone who didn't know better would think it's all about the clothes. It's not entirely about the clothes, but what's the point of rowing and being in shape if you can't show it off with cute attire?

We are a crew of seven. Invariably, a few are on vacation or have a wedding, funeral, house showing, or graduation. We need a few extras to fill the quad on these occasions. We are not fussy about which seat we row, but only two of us can bow.

Bowing is only a coveted position if you are into telling people what to do. It's hard work. Not only do you row, but you must keep a keen eye out for what's sneaking up behind and call for the crew to help turn by asking for port or starboard pressure. The crew responds to this request by pushing harder with one leg than the other. Often it is easier for the bow to turn the boat themselves than to call for help all the time, which takes a physical toll.

Most people don't like to bow. Some are scared to be responsible for the crew's safety; some are lazy. Most people who do bow have pretty much just fallen into the position. They must be brave or full of the damn-the-torpe-does-full-steam-ahead bravado and not averse to taking on a little extra effort.

Each bow has a different style. Some, like me, are gentle. I'm always careful to say thank you when asking the crew to do something special. My calls are definitive and loud but not chastising or demanding. No matter where I sit in a boat, I'm after the magic that rowing induces. When I bow, I can encourage that state.

We usually begin with a slow, easy warm-up, breathing in the simple juiciness of being on the water, basking in the sunshine, and catching a glimpse of egret, heron, or osprey. The crew might chat amicably for the first few minutes. These women are generally not fast friends off the river. We often move in circles where we might occasionally meet, but something quite unlike anything else happens on the river.

These mature women, transformed by marriage, children, and death, are bonded in their ancient archetype. If we set aside our egos for a moment and look deeply into each other's eyes, we see ourselves. Something about this shared life experience allows us to sync and flow naturally.

We don't talk about this. We don't need to. If my crew were asked to think about this, they might roll their eyes and wonder what I was smoking. But, somewhere in their souls, they will hear what I am saying whisper in their psyche and recognize its truth.

In this familiar space, women can be lulled by the rhythm and sounds of the stroke. Our audible chatter might be about working on technique, per-fecting our blade work, slowing our slide, crisping up our catch, and leaning back at the finish. But we simultaneously allow the nymphs to pull us into that space where we recognize our feminine roles as caregivers, life givers, and nurturers. In this timeless void, we act as one in that boat, our hands doing their work, our legs theirs, and our thoughts carried off on the wind.

Sometimes, especially in the spring, I think about keeping my blade just below the water on the drive. And that concentration will be interrupted by the smell of the Russian olive's sweet, cloying smell wafting upon the river's ripples, tantalizing the cilia inside my nose and taking me to another dimension. In other moments, my reverie might be induced by reminding my toes to slowly pull me up the slide. But that focus gently morphs into a luscious puddle of being at the sound of a goose honking. And with all this distraction, I'm working without effort in sync with my crew. These suspensions of time take me to that core of my aliveness and oneness with my crew and all that lives.

When a crew works at peak effort, the mind is adept at blocking out thoughts other than those necessary to propel that boat ahead. Often there are simply no thoughts at all. Muscle memory takes over, and we are free to roam the seas of sensuality and rhythm on the waves of strength and speed.

On the other hand, some of us row for the workout, the competitive high, the mastery of the water and oar. These women don't allow this siren song to take them where it wants them to go. Often these women are younger athletes, driven at all they do in their lives, unslowed yet by their grown children exercising their own minds or by life's devastating disappointments. Some only need to be in control, not allowing themselves the wonder of riding that space without time.

One of our crew members is competitive, demanding, and loud on and off the water. She often referred to herself as "bitch" and didn't get along well with everyone, and especially not with anyone who likes to take control.

It's no surprise, then, that Lauren liked to bow. I think of her as the Gestapo. I heard her heels click sharply together when she gave a command. Or maybe it was me and some of the other crew members I heard clicking the heels of our red shoes, hoping to escape back to Kansas.

"Okay, girrrrlllls, let's get this baby down. Hands-on, up and out," she would say.

It's normally up to the bow to "call" the boat down to the dock, which means to state the commands so that everyone does it together. This instruction was to get the quad off its rack and carry it overhead.

Lauren was a talker, constantly adding more than a few chuckles to a row. She was a push-me, pull-me person. My experience was that she sometimes went out of her way to be kind and thoughtful, but the effort was not consistent. She reached out but never pulled you in close enough to establish even a rented parking space in her neighborhood. It was not always easy to feel close to her.

Once at the dock, "Overhead and in. Okay, ladies, let's get going and get on the water quick. We must be back by 10:00. I'll bow."

There was no discussion of who would bow. There never was; she decided if it would be her or me. If looks were groans at the news of her bowing, they would be heard in the next town. Her rows were demanding and anxiety-provoking. We would steel ourselves for the inevitable.

Out on the water at our first bridge, Lauren barks. "Hard starboard NOW!"

With that, our stroke rate doubles, and we push hard on our right legs like our lives depend upon it, thinking that indeed they do since a call that fierce can mean only that we are in imminent danger of collision with something.

"Even," she calls. That means we can return to a regular row and are no longer in danger of going down like the Hindenburg. As we pass through the bridge, it's clear that there was no emergency. It's just Lauren's style.

I hear Deb mumble behind me, "Damn, I thought we were about to crash into a piling. Why all the shouting?"

"Okay, are we ready for some work? Let's do a power 30 in 2."

It's not a democracy, so the question is rhetorical. In two strokes, we are pushing as hard as we can for thirty strokes.

Lauren gives us a minute or so of paddling break and then says, "In two, we're going to increase the stroke rate by two."

And Deb behind me, "Aren't we going fast enough? I want a nice, easy row. Damn."

Teri, our squeaky-voiced boat boy seeker, is rowing stroke and diligently increases our rate by two strokes a minute.

"The boys do this for an hour without a break," Lauren says. She refers to a quad of men she bows for who really like a good workout.

"We are not the boys," I mutter.

Lauren continues to call for stroke rate increases until our technique sucks because we are going so fast and can't stay in sync. Finally, someone asks for a water break, and we stop.

We are at a railroad bridge, and the train is approaching, "Okay, girls, make it look like you're pulling the cord on a whistle, and let's see if he will do it for us. Altogether, pull," Lauren bellows.

The engineer sees us mimicking, pulling the cord, and blows his whistle.

"Ah," Lauren laughs, "he loves us. Do it again. One two three, pull."

We all fake pull, and he blows it again.

"I can't belieeeeve he's doooiiiing that," Teri says.

By now, Lauren is beside herself, and we are all laughing with her.

"That's pretty cool," says Deb.

"Okay, let's row, ladies."

And we are off again.

At our next water break, Teri says, "I just had a thought. "We should figure out a way to tie up the quad to the dock at Up the Creek so we can hop in for lunch. Wouldn't that be fun?"

Up the Creek was a dive restaurant/bar at the confluence of the Brandywine and Christina rivers. It was old, decrepit, sold terrible food, watered-down drinks, and everyone loved it. It was a cult thing. Guitar, banjo, and fiddle players would show up and jam on Wednesday nights. They would mostly play Country and Western, so it was a great place to show up in your cowboy boots and hat. It was on our rowing path going downriver, so we would pass it often. It did have a dock out front, but we never saw any boats moored there. Maybe in the past days, they did a good business from people coming up the Delaware in boats and turning into the Christina. It was very close to the Delaware River Port.

"There is no way to do that, Teri," I respond, rolling my eyes at yet another of Teri's schemes!

"Well, if we got some good nylon rope and tied it from the dock to the center of the riggers, tucking the port oars under the dock, it might work. What do ya'all think?"

Lauren is laughing along with the rest of us, "You know, Teri, I have a jar at home with a sticker that says Teri's Good Ideas. It's full. One of these days, I'll give it to you."

As the season rolls on, our crew gets in better shape and likes a bit of a harder workout, and Lauren mellows some to the pace of the rest of us. Sometimes, we even ask her to keep it to a dull roar, and she does. And sometimes I bow and all is a bit more relaxed.

"Ready all, and row," Lauren shouts. "What shall we do on the way back? Let's do a pyramid. In two . . ."

And we are off and running to another fire somewhere.

CHAPTER 23

It's All About Me

I was fascinated by Lauren. She was beautiful, a good athlete, a leader, and fun and she was the glue that held our morning quad together. She played the role of mother hen, coaching us in the ways of the world (of men especially), scolding us if we didn't do right, and pushing us to be our best. She held our family of female rec rowers together with gaiety and laughter.

Every man who met her was just a little bit in love with her, and maybe some of the women too. She had that kind of charisma. We all adored her. If *Readers Digest* was still publishing, she would be my entry for My Most Unforgettable Character. I wanted to be her; the next best thing was being her friend.

Yes, Lauren was relentless in the bow seat of her quad, shouting commands, making us rush along, and demanding gut-busting workouts. "It's all about me," she would cackle as she yelled at us to hurry it up.

Not only did she command our quad from the bow seat, but she also served as our leader. Lauren organized us, scheduled us, and kept us laughing. She regaled us with her dating stories of what qualified men, in her book, as absolute rejects. The 90/10 rule was #1. Oh, yes, they were all numbered!

"Most men talk about themselves profusely on the first date." she declares. "If they don't talk about you at least 10 percent of the time, they are goners."

And then, "So we were driving for a tee time (a good sign, he was a golfer), and I noticed he drove the car with hands on the wheel at 10 and 2 o'clock. Ugh." This is #23, as I recall, but my retention of these numbers was not great; there were so many to remember.

"What's wrong with that," asks Deb.

"Too staid, unimaginative, predictable," is her answer.

Huh?

And another reject: "So, we were on our second date. He had passed the obvious rules. We walked by a ball and chain at this historic site in Chester. He said, "Looks like someone tossed off that marriage." What the hell? That ended him."

She told us about the bad breath rule #75 from the bow one morning. "The one I met Friday night was a loser. As soon as he stepped toward me to say hello, I wanted to shout 'HALITOSIS alert.' Didn't he brush his teeth or gargle before meeting a prospective date? What an idiot!"

"Hey, maybe he was just following the keto diet and breathing out ketones," Deb suggested.

Changing the subject, "Oh my god, did you see that," she screamed. "We just passed a toothbrush floating on the port side!"

"No," I said. "You're making it up."

"Hold water," she shouted. "Look right. There, see it?"

"Where?"

"Two o'clock! It's blue, bristles side up!"

"Oh shit, you weren't kidding. Waiiiitttt. Did you just throw that in," asked Teri.

"No. Why would I be rowing with a toothbrush? See, even the river gods agree that halitosis is a date killer!"

It took five minutes of amazement and laughter before we could resume the row.

The rules (and they were numbered) were to ensure that no slight misstep went unnoticed. But above all else, rule #48 was the most important: "Never sleep with them until you've dated for six weeks."

"Since they have waited so long, anticipation and excitement are high. They won't notice the sagging rolls pocked with cellulite that come with sixty-year-old bodies."

She might have broken this rule at least once. She was rowing sweep with a crew called "The Motleys," such was their rowing performance. One of them invited a friend from Baltimore to row with them one Friday night and to join them for dinner afterward at a local Italian place.

Well, the minute Dick, voted the most eligible bachelor in Baltimore, showed up in his spandex, we women all noticed. He was either generously endowed or stuffing his jock strap under his spandex with hiking socks. Lauren, of course, saw first and had that bright one-hundred-watt smile ready for him. He asked her if she was free to go out the following night. No mustache, halitosis, or violation of the 90/10 rule. She was in.

"Yuperdoo," she responded.

What happened on that date has yet to be discovered. Dick's story, as relayed to his buddies, was that she "jumped his bones." Hmm, really, or just bragging about his ability to get her into bed on the first date?

On the other hand, she told the ladies he "jumped her bones," and she didn't have a chance with that package. Really? Or maybe she was bragging that she experienced what the rest of us lusted after if it actually happened. At the very least, she had to admit she broke her own six-week rule and insisted he didn't seem to mind. Funny, though, it was a one-night affair. And that was the first and last time we saw Dick.

One morning, from the bow, she bellowed, "Pass the lubricant! I'm not twenty-one anymore," for no good reason except that it occurred to her at that moment.

We once challenged her to be quiet for the entire row. She didn't much like it, but she did comply. It was the only time the boat was silent with her in it.

On another day.

"Okay girlllssss, face right and smile. Someone on shore is taking our picture."

She knew she had a beautiful smile. If a camera or an admirer were anywhere nearby, she'd face them with a smile that lit up her face. She smiled a lot. She loved cameras, and they loved her. There were many photos of that smile. In fact, every last one of her photos featured that "aren't I a knock-out smile?". How did she manage not to have those candid photos where the rest of us look so awful that we try to declare it's not us, we were having a bad hair day, or we hate having our picture taken because they never look like us? Lauren never needed an excuse. Not one lousy photo. Nope.

During a rest break, she taught us about the queenly wave. "Ever notice how the queen raises her arm and twists it at the wrist to create her friendly wave instead of waggling it around? That's so that that loose skin hanging under her arm doesn't flop around and remind people how old she is. Mark my word, ladies, the queenly wave will keep them from guessing your age! Do it now," she would insist, and we would all comply, waving merrily from our boat at nothing.

The men's recreational quad frequently called her if they needed a substitute bow. They would say they asked her because she wasn't shy about a good workout. Who were they kidding? They loved looking at the pretty smile and languishing in her vibrant personality.

She was always the life of the party and commanded the center of attention. And she engendered intrigue by always rushing to go somewhere important. She made a living as a real estate agent. But she was an avid golfer, tennis player, Mexican train player, rower, and active volunteer for her church. To fit all this in, she was always in a hurry. Her reach was broad in the small town in which she lived. And everyone she touched enjoyed her smile and her humor.

I often found myself trying to be clever and witty around her. I craved her attention and wanted her to be my friend. Such was her magnetism. Other times, I argued with her but always succumbed to what she wanted. Such was her need to have her way.

After our morning rows, she often insisted we go for coffee at the local café. It was a great chance to catch up on each other's lives outside the rows. After some chit-chat, she would interrupt, demanding that we tell her which of the guys on her dating sites (and she used them all) she should respond to.

"What do you think of this one?" she asked as she showed us pictures of the available options on her phone.

"He looks cute," someone would reply.

"Yeah, but he's got that mustache. Do you think he's hiding something, maybe skinny, unkissable lips? How about this one," she said as she swiped to another she had found on a different dating site. There were always several choices.

Sometimes I wonder if she had difficulty concentrating. She frequently jumped from one thought to another, one hobby to another, one man to another.

She followed up on the mustache one for a coffee date, but he didn't pass the 90/10 rule. She did not respond when he tried to communicate with her after their "date," but he did find out where she lived and texted her one night that he was outside and waiting to see her. Of course, she freaked and called her always-reliable friend Herbie. He showed up and told the guy Lauren was his girlfriend and that he, Herbie, was a member of the town's mafia.

Herbie and Lauren, at one point, dated. They both loved golf and were very social partygoers. They were the attractive couple on the scene of all charity events in our town, knowing everyone who was anyone. For whatever reason, she tired of him or maybe was afraid of not tiring of him and so they subsequently become friends. He was always there for her and forever in love with her.

There was one guy she stuck with for a few months. She even brought him around to some boat club activities. We all liked him just fine. He was good-looking, had no mustache, brushed and gargled, didn't drive in the 10 o'clock or 2 o'clock position, had a great physique, was a couple (or maybe a few) years younger than her, and had a terrific personality. We were surprised and disappointed that he didn't last.

"He wants to stay home sometimes and be just with me," she declared.

"Sounds like he just wants more of you to himself instead of sharing you with all your friends all the time," Deb said.

"Hey, I like my friends, and if he doesn't want to spend time with them, then he's not for me." Compromise on this issue was not in her paradigm.

According to her, she has had 256 dates since her divorce. She, therefore, considered herself an expert on dating, thus the "rules." I was convinced she was terrified to try a steady relationship again. Her husband divorced her and then promptly hung himself, leaving her on her own to raise their two kids. That's gotta make a mother wary.

One of our club members decided it would be fun to hold a fundraiser for the Wilmington Breakfast Mission. We would all dress up in Christmas costumes, raise money from our friends and family, and row a few miles on a designated Saturday just before Christmas. And, cheekily enough, there would be medals for the best costumes. Yippee.

"Common girrlllsss, let's get together to figure out what to wear. We are gonna win first place for our costumes and raise the most funds," from Lauren.

The morning rec quad and the Panthers banded together to form a sweep boat for the Santa row. Every week or two, we met to figure out our first-place winning costumes and then fabricate them. Over the years, we created costumes as gingerbread men, reindeer, candy canes, snow angels (all white fleece with wings and sparkly headbands with protruding blingy white balls bobbing over our heads), poinsettias (dressed in all green, draped in plastic poinsettia flowers, and all of us crouched into a circle of gold mylar simulating a pot from which we emerged while someone watered us with a blinged-up three-gallon watering can and we all sang "Feliz Navidad"), jingle bell rock and rollers (picture poodle skirts with Christmas trees instead of poodles and a toy jukebox that played jingle bell rock as we jitterbugged in our black duct-taped white tennis shoes designed to mimic saddle shoes), and Christmas cowboys. We always added a little drama to our costumes with some performance.

One year we dressed as clowns in red and green PJs, ruffs made from a child's red tutu, and elaborate clown makeup. We tied one hundred balloons to our sweep boat. What's a clown without balloons? Lowering our oars to take a stroke, we were baffled by being unable to move the boat one millimeter, no matter how hard we pushed. Red and green balloons bobbed on the water draped from the gunnels of our boat, looking spectacular, but the drag they created rendered the boat immobile. We punctured all those balloons we had spent hours blowing up just to pull away from the dock. Oh well. It was quite a site as long as we didn't try to row.

Whenever we got frustrated with an idea, Lauren would push to find a way around whatever barrier we faced in getting our costumes together. When we thought we were through developing our costumes, Lauren would find something else to add. As with rowing, she pushed us and made us better. And sometimes, I think she just wanted to continue to meet socially or maybe have the last word.

On Christmas row day, there were many clever costumes besides ours. Ours were just always better. Half the club would show up to row or help keep the boat traffic flowing by working on the dock, cooking sausages, making mimosas, taking photos and videos of the event, passing out medals, introducing the Brother from the mission who had been sent to judge the best costumes and collect the check from the money we raised. It never amounted to more than a few thousand. One year, we managed $11,000. But the Breakfast Mission always supported the event and appreciated anything we raised.

We won first place every single year. These were the only medals we ever won, not being racers.

All came to a crashing halt with the call on Christmas Day.

It was Linda. "We lost Lauren," she whispered.

"What do you mean we lost her?" I asked.

"Her son found her in her bedroom last night, gone."

"What? No. Impossible."

"Oh my god. How?"

"No one knows yet. She was on the floor in her nightgown."

But there it was, our hero, our leader, our Nazi, our friend, gone just like that at sixty-two. How could the world go on without her? How could we?

Her memorial was held after Christmas. Even, or maybe, especially in death, she did not want people looking at her without that radiating smile. Her casket was closed. It was better this way. We wouldn't have recognized her without the smile and the laugh.

There were at least five hundred people who came to show respect for her life and share sadness at her death. Almost every member of our boat club was there. I had never, and probably will never, see anything else like it. She was known, remembered, revered, and loved by so many.

A week later, all her female crew members met at the river. I made some plastic gadgets to hold candles and any tokens we wanted her to have to help her cross the River Styx. We lit and floated these on the tide of the Christina in her honor. We peppered the river with two dozen pink and white long-stemmed American Beauty roses.

We sang her off with love songs and songs that she loved and tried to say goodbye. Many of us still remember her on Christmas Eve with a toast to wherever she is, missing her radiant presence.

In our last Santa row, we dressed as Christmas cowboys again, but with her picture on our backs in her honor for all the years she got us to first place. She was a one-of-a-kind, brilliant light, the likes of which this world will not see again. And she was right; it was always all about her.

CHAPTER 24

Bladders on the Water

A row normally lasts anywhere from forty minutes to a couple of hours. Anything less than that obviates all the aggravation of getting the boat down, rigged up, and then cleaning and putting it away afterwards. Anything more than that and a glorious row can become an exercise in physical torture.

Unlike sturdy kayaks and canoes, fragile sculls cannot be casually dragged out of the water onto to the river's edge. Even singles cost quite a few thousand dollars, and the hulls are not made to be scraped along dirt, stones and roots. Unlike power and cruise boats there is simply no way to tie a scull to a dock and expect it to stay upright. These shortcomings translate into no beer stops, junk food runs, or bathroom breaks.

Rowing is primarily a warm weather sport and requires a lot of exertion, resulting in buckets of sweat. Dehydration is a danger, so most rowers keep at least a quart of water in the boat to frequently replenish the body's wrung-out cells. And, as any warm weather sport enthusiast will tell you, you know you are hydrated only when your bladder tells you. So rowers face a conundrum.

I often wonder if the men who engage in long, earnest, sweaty workouts have found a way to use their convenient built-in equipment in response to the bladder demands. I knew a salesman once who claimed he never had to make rest stops on long trips. He insisted that he could hold the car door open while driving down a superhighway and not get a drop on the door or his pants. I reasoned that similar principles could be applied here. But in this case, fear of drops in the cockpit (no pun intended) that you later will turn upside down over your head might be a deterrent.

There was a group of older gentlemen calling themselves the Quad Squad who would not allow bottles of water aboard during their rows. It wasn't that they didn't sweat, but that they all had prostate issues, giving them the "tiny bladder" syndrome so often attributed to women. Did they make the "drink no water aboard" rule because men really can't manage the maneuver from the boat, or because they were no longer confident of their ability to keep the cockpit dry in the process?

We had lots of forty-something male rowers in our club, and I never once caught one of them in the middle of the act. Of course it's not like you can creep up on someone in a scull. The potential offender would see any intruder long before they were close enough to be detected. So the mystery remains: can they or can't they?

Women can't. This I know. There is a device sold by outdoor stores called Freshet that I tried once while camping. We were heading out to white-water raft the Rio Generales in Costa Rica, and my husband had convinced me that snakes there could kill you with one bite. Consequently, I was no longer comfortable having to leave the tent in the middle of the night upon my bladder's demand.

This Freshet gizmo was a combination of a funnel appliance attached to a short length of hose that fit into a plastic bag, which could be sealed after use and disposed of. I took it with me but unfortunately found it a bit unreliable, much to my tentmate's chagrin.

Most women I row with make a point of visiting the bathroom just before going out on the water. I was not always among the ranks of the cautious but had my coming home to Jesus moment that converted me.

It was my fourth season of sculling, and I was out on a lovely summer morning with a buddy. We rowed our singles almost daily that summer during her teaching break. Since our river had its perils, the two of us liked to go out together in the event that one or the other of us got in some kind of trouble. I was generally out in front but kept her in sight with my Roy Orbison spy sunglasses.

Maybe a half hour into our row, the urge struck. Usually I can ignore these demands, and I did for another fifteen minutes or so. But there would be no denying long enough to row my way back to the boathouse in time this time. I considered my options. I could pull an oar alongside the scull and tip over to resolve the issue, but that would require immersion in that horrid, slime-populated river. I could, since I was already sweat-drenched, just let it happen. But the horror of what I would endure when I turned the boat upside down over my head to carry it into the boathouse scotched that notion in a heartbeat.

I opted to head for the public boat launch just a mile or so upriver. It was closer than the boathouse, was sure to be outfitted with a public restroom, and had a slanted shore free of stones where I could pull the scull close to shore, and since it was a protected area, I needn't worry that the tide would squire it downstream. Decision was made. Barb was too far behind me to let her know of my desperation, so I had to leave her in my wake as she happily moseyed along. She would have to fend for herself. This was a penultimate emergency.

I made like a Cape Canaveral rocket for the boat launch. A galley slave in the hold of my own ship, mindlessly following the pound of a silent stroke beater, I pulled against the water. Each stroke was agony, my breath came in gulps, my legs drove my seat back harder and farther than reasonable, my stroke rate crept up to a racing rate of thirty, my heart rate an edgy 180, my oars dug deeply into the sludgy waters and splashed wildly at the stroke finish. Each plunge of blade and arch forward threatened to unbalance me and my scull and dip us into the chemically effluent waters. Finally, I arrived.

Rowing in close enough to step out ankle deep and pull the scull up to keep it at the shoreline, I clambered lightning fast out of the boat and barely noticed a guy fishing at the end of the dock. Too shy and embarrassed to ask about the whereabouts of the public restroom, I simply ran up the ramp in the direction where I assumed it would be.

It was not there. It was not anywhere. Panic. A quick look around and unrelenting urgency convinced me that it was time to drop my drawers and duck behind a tree. Relief. I took just a moment to sigh and catch my breath before struggling to quickly pull up my now very sweat-soaked sticky spandex lest the fisherman come strolling by.

Attempting to affect the nonchalance of someone who had some legitimate, important business at the launch site, I slowly strode back to the shore, found my scull where I had left it, and ignored the curious glance from the fisherman. I could not think of one good explanation to offer him for my obvious behavior. I was surprised he didn't snicker.

Thinking that from now on I might consider visiting the restroom before shoving off from the boathouse dock, I met Barb and went on to have a very uneventful row. It was a day or two before I started to itch. It was just a little at first, easily ignored. But after a couple of days, agony prevailed.

I suffered a week of sleepless days and nights either itching, scratching, and blistering or unsuccessfully trying to ignore the incessant itching and maddening need to scratch. There were brief moments when I found relief with various potions, lotions, and unguents. But it was no real relief since it was during those times when I became anxious about facing the inevitable madness of the itch again.

Thoughts alternated between cutting off my hands so I couldn't scratch and the horror of not having hands to relieve the crazed itching. I would shake my hands from the wrist to keep them busy doing something besides scratching and at the same time squiggle and squirm around in my seat to affect some satisfaction for the itch. There was no respite. Defeated, I finally dragged myself to the doctor begging for relief.

Not only had I managed to get poison ivy on my butt and thighs, but apparently on my hands as well because there were lines of blisters where I had struggled to pull the spandex up over my hips. The sweat added its two cents by assisting the spread around the waistband of my shorts.

Doc declared it was one of the worst cases he had seen and shook his finger at me, saying if I had come in right away he could have prevented all this aggravation, but at this point there was nothing he could do.

Wallowing in my suffering, I returned home to face the torture for another few days before it began to let up, and during one lucid moment, I committed to make the boathouse restrooms my last stop before a row. It's a rule I do not break.

CHAPTER 25

We Come in Many Flavors

Rowing is a great whole-body exercise. Lean and well-defined legs are the norm, and shorts are back in the wardrobe. Strong shoulder muscles develop, making wearing those cute little backless tops attractive again. Back and abdominal muscles play an important role as well. The flat stomach, which most of us haven't seen since teenage years, comes back. And, especially important for women, the butt gets tight. You can wear flats and get the effect of wearing four-inch spikes. That alone was enough to convince me.

My body by fifty-five was better than it had ever been, including all the countless times I joined gyms, aerobic, yoga, Zumba, kickboxing, spinning, and on and on classes. Of course, some of that difference might have been because my tenacity at those classes was less than stellar. But the thing that makes me happiest is that the couch potato I had been most of my life emerged into the athlete who had been there and been ignored all along.

Adding better news is, barring injury, surgery, or major back or shoulder problems, rowers row till they drop. We had a seventy-three-year-old do just that after coming in from a row. His wife, who is also a rower, says, "That's the way he would have chosen to go if he had had the choice." It might have been okay for the two of them to have him have that heart attack on the water, but it sure freaked the rest of us out.

And racers are true diehards; I once helped an eighty-year-old man steady himself to get out of his double scull after participating in a race. It didn't matter to him or his fans that he crossed the finish line moments before the next heat of racers caught up with him. We almost hoped he might have had a fleeting memory of what it was like to win a race since he was ahead of the boats from the next race. He may not have the power he once had, but his stroke was graceful and technique perfect—a pleasure and inspiration to behold.

We had a woman in our club who started rowing at fourteen and rowed to eight-four. She rowed stroke seat in sweep, and everyone in the club helped get her boat down to the dock. Miss Lydia was serious about her rows. If her crew stood around chatting, she expressed her impatience: "Are ve going to row today or yust talk?" she would ask in a thick German accent she never lost. It was amusing to watch this skinny, wrinkled old lady assume a hands-on hip posture to get her crew onto the water.

She was short, painfully thin, and in those later years, her parchment skin began to hang precariously from bony limbs. She gave the impression that a not-so-stiff wind might just whoosh her away at any moment. But she was far from meek. When she coxed a crew, she complained bitterly if the boat was not set. "Quit the viggle vaggling" (which means "stop listing from side to side") she would wail.

I watched her once shake her finger and yell in German at someone who had committed some perceived sin or another, her thin voice whiney and whispery in its delivery. But that wagging finger told another story, even to the appropriately chagrined six-foot-four gentleman who was on the receiving end of her wrath.

One time I was rowing with her and two sixty-somethings in a quad. All of us had a fair amount of experience and were good rowers. Our bow had cut one turn a little too tight, and we went aground on a sandbar. We all thought it was so funny that we had to just sit there and chuckle about it for a minute.

"Did we run aground?" asked Sue?

"Yup," Gail laughed. "Sandbar moved since last year."

I teased, "Ah, I don't think so. I think our bow just wasn't paying attention."

"I'm so sorry. I couldn't see it, and it has come way out into the river since last fall," Sue apologetically proclaimed.

We were all so busy passing jibes and laughing at this situation that we didn't even notice our Lydia get out of the boat and step into the muck in an attempt to pull our boat off the sandbar. The sight of her old, wizened, skinny body tugging at the boat with us three loads still in it sent us even further into gales of laughter.

"God, Lydia, get back in the boat," Gail roared.

Sue, stifling a laugh, said, "Oh dear. Lydia, be careful."

I was doubled over with laughter and between gulps for air said, "I can't believe we are sitting here watching the eighty-year-old pull our butts off the bottom!"

The more Lydia mumbled and tugged, sunk into the muck, and fell into the water, the more we laughed and were physically unable to get control enough to get out of the boat to help her. As far as she was concerned, someone had to get us off that sandbar, and she didn't see any of us doing it.

CHAPTER 26

No Bunions Allowed

It was April, and rowing season was about to start. Weather was warming, March winds had died down, and April showers were diminishing. And I had a horrible bunion brought on by years of wearing pointed-toed, high-heeled shoes. Even though my feet sometimes hurt, I persisted in wearing these every day at work during my thirties, even when wearing my white lab coat. I walked a mile each way to and from the subway to get to my clinical lab in those puppies. Surprised my toes didn't fuse into one pointed appendage.

Was I crazy or what? Noooo, just following the fad at the time. And everyone knows heels make your butt look perky. Ah, the price we pay for beauty.

But at sixty, the piper was calling and had to be paid. I had this ugly bunion. I once showed it to a friend who murmured, "ew" upon seeing it; it was that bad. Embarrassed to wear sandals, I figured it was time to do something about it. Doc said surgery to correct it was no problem as long as I didn't mind walking around in one of those clunky black postsurgical shoes for a couple of weeks. I didn't mind doing THAT, but I did mind missing rows.

Hating to give up rowing, I scheduled the surgery for late May. That way I could get in almost two months of rowing. Doc assured me I could walk immediately and would be in the surgical shoe no more than four weeks after surgery. I would be back in stroke seat sometime in July. Sounded reasonable.

I gloriously rowed all May, did surgery at the end of that month.

One May row just before surgery, Ann asked, "Is it okay if Colleen rows with us during your recovery?"

Colleen was a sub when someone of us had to miss. She was a decent rower. But she always referred to us as "gals." "Good row, gals." "You gals want to go for coffee?" "Thanks, gals, see you tomorrow."

For me it was like fingernail scratches on a blackboard. Made me wince. Weird prejudice, I know.

"Of course," I crooned, not really meaning it. I hated the thought that someone, anyone else was rowing routinely with MY crew. But everyone assured me that my seat was still my seat. Colleen would row three seat and Ann would stroke.

"Danielle, stroke in our boat will always be your seat. We can't wait till you are healed and back in it with us. We will miss you," declared Lou.

"But Colleen is a good rower and you will be great in stroke," I whined to Ann.

"Don't be ridiculous, stroke seat is yours. I'd much rather row behind you. And Colleen is okay, but she is not a Panther."

"We would never give your seat to anyone, Danielle. You are irreplaceable in our crew. Stop worrying," reassured Linda.

Did that stop me from worrying? Of course not. I was hurt. Unreasonably so. But still.

When "my crew" decided to race at Diamond States with Colleen in the boat, I just about lost it. It's one thing to use a sub for me when I couldn't row, but I was healed by race day. I just hadn't rowed with my crew again yet, and to jump into the boat at this point would be a disservice to my three crewmates. And there was the fact that my crew frequently expressed interest in racing at least one race each year. And each year I demurred because with my diminished lung capacity racing was a brutal task. But still.

On race day, I helped them "hot seat," meaning the boat they were to race in was docking from another race, and the crews that had just raced had to get out so my crew could get into the boat. I wished them luck as they left the launch dock for the start, and I proceeded to the finish line to watch the race. One after another the competitors finished to the blare of the finish horn. My crew was nowhere to be seen.

The problem began even before they got into the boat. The boat they were to hot seat was the last one to finish their race. As such it took a long time for boats finishing before them to clear the takeout dock at the finish line. Once that crew got into the dock, took out their oars, and got out of that boat, my crew had to get in, attach their oars, adjust shoes, and take off. The start was a much farther row from the finish dock than the launch dock from which all other competitors in this race were rowing.

All this means that my crew was late for the start and the referee starters decided not to wait. The other crews were racing the course while my crew was still trying to get to the start. Consequently, my crew rowed the course alone, all other crews in that race being at 750 meters when they managed to start. Couldn't have gone much more wrong.

My crew had been excited about the race and expectedly disappointed. Worst of all, it wasn't really their fault. Not to be expected, however, was that Colleen was livid, mumbling disparaging words as she exited the boat. Don't know if she was angry at anyone in particular or just at the outcome in general. Maybe she was just embarrassed having dragged her husband to the race to watch. I was back in the boat that July in stroke seat. All was right in my world.

CHAPTER 27

Octopussy on the Lake

"I'd like to race again at Diamond States, ladies," Linda announces on a break during a row.

"Argh," I moaned, not again. This had come up before. All three of my crewmates wanted just one race every year. "I can't manage even five minutes of full-out effort with my damn COPD. You have to find another stroke seat."

"No," Linda emphatically replied, "we are not racing with anybody else in stroke. And you do the fastest starts I've ever seen."

"Yeah, my starts and the fifteen high strokes following are great, but I'm done by the time we finish those. I'm a great 250-meter sprinter, but the race is one thousand meters. I don't have the breath."

"I have a great idea. What if we race an octopod (an eight-person scull)? There is no heat for octopods so that we would be the only ones in the race; we could take our time moseying down the lake and win a first-place medal AND trophy," giggles Ann.

"Linda chimes in, "that is a great idea, Ann."

"Do you think the club would let us do it and establish a race just for us?" I ask warily. "And anyway, we don't have an octopod."

"We could see if Hans would rerig one of our eights from a sweep to scull. We could easily get four of the Santa Row gang to join us," Lou suggests.

"That would be a hoot," from Ann.

"I guess I could do that," I say warily.

"Of course you can," assures Lou. You stroke at any rate you want, and we follow. The point is not to beat anyone since we would be the only boat in the race. Yahoo." She sings, "We are going to race at Diamond States. We are going to race at the Diamond States. He, he, he, that rhymes!"

"God Lou, you are so funny," Linda tells her.

"I bet Fran would be willing to cox an all-woman octopod. She would love that," I suggest. "Okay, I'm in! Panthers Rule!"

Diamond States Masters Regatta is a race sponsored yearly by our boat club on a small lake a little south of our town. It is the last masters, aka adults, race before the coveted Nationals. It's when serious teams racing at Nationals get to stand off against each other and get a taste of each other's mettle. The venue is also a favorite. It's a lake surrounded by grass and trees instead of a crowded river, and racers bring families and tents and make a picnic outing of the day.

A couple of days later, "Lay hold, overhead and up. To shoulders and down," from Lou. "I talked to Hans about rigging an eight to an octopod, and he told me that St. Andrew's [the boys boarding school and lake where *Dead Poets Society* was filmed that we use for our masters regatta in July] had one rigged as an octopod. He said he was sure we could use it for that race. No one else uses it."

"Oh my god. That's perfect," I tell her as we walk the boat down to the water.

"Overhead and up, toe to edge, roll 'er in ladies."

For the next few minutes, we get oars, move shoes, put gear into the bottom of the boat, and complain about our day.

Linda says, "I warned them to get travel insurance, but they didn't listen. Last night I got the call around midnight. 'My son just broke his leg. I need to get him back to the States ASAP. Can you get us a private jet?'" Linda is a travel agent by day and, in this case, by night.

"Gee, Linda, it sounds like they take advantage of you. Why didn't you tell them to get a private jet on their own," from Ann, who adds, "Who rowed this boat today? The shoes are soaked.

"They think this is part of what they get when they use a travel agent, and most of the time, I don't mind, but MIDNIGHT. Come on. . . ."

"The log says it was Rosemary's quad. They're good rowers. They shouldn't be splashing. Wonder if they went over?" says Lou.

"So what did you do, Linda?" I ask.

"I called MEDJET to get him and his son back to Delaware. Going to cost him $25,000. Think he will get insurance next time?"

"Wow, I can't believe he would pay that. He was in France, right? Don't they have decent health care? It was just a broken leg, right?" Ann says.

"Port oars out, one foot in and down," calls Lou.

Putting on her shoes, fastening Velcro, and sitting up straight, Linda says with disdain, "It's not like he can't afford the jet. It just makes me mad that he didn't listen to me and had the nerve to call me at midnight to fix his problem."

"He was probably beside himself with his son writhing in agony next to him," I reason. "Maybe next time, tell him to lose your phone number?"

"Yeah, fat chance of that happening. I have to quit this job! Time to retire." And with that, "One hand on the dock and shove."

We do our workout, and at the break, "So Hans says Saint Andrew's School has an octopod already rigged that we can use for the race."

"Yippee!" from Lou.

"Okay, all we have to do is call four others to row with us," I add.

"I'll ask Fran to cox. I'm sure she will," says Linda.

Ann adds, "I'll call Teri and Harriett."

"I can try Colleen and Nancy," I add as well.

"There we go, ladies, our first first-place medal at the Diamond States," shouts Lou! "We need to get back to the boathouse. It's getting late. Sit at the finish, ready all, our start and row."

And many strokes later, "Oh my god, ladies, we will call the boat the Octopussy! Ha-ha. We are all women, including the cox," laughs Linda.

No one called "waynuf," but we stopped rowing anyway. We were laughing too hard to keep going.

We did a practice row on Noxontown Pond and surprised ourselves by being in sync! The boat was loaned to us by St. Andrew's, the school that rowed on the pond during the school year, and was used for our club's annual regatta. It had been unused and ignored for years. Things creaked and whined, and it was an old heavyweight, but it rowed. And anyhow, we didn't need a great boat to win since we wouldn't have competition. Well, wasn't that just magical thinking?

It turns out that after we convinced our club to let us race an octopod, they decided to offer it as a legitimate race for anyone to enter. They could have done us the favor of waiting until the last minute to list it, but they fancied additional registration fees wherever possible. One crew from another club had raced octopods before and was delighted we created a race for them—so much for our clever plan to win a medal.

Undaunted, we carried forth. "What the heck. It will be fun anyway," from Ann.

"Yeah, right," I grumbled.

So, we got to the school to pick up the octopod. "Hi, we're here to pick up your octopod," I said to some guy hanging around.

"Yeah. I got the word you were borrowing it."

"Can you show us where you have it racked? It was there a couple of weeks ago when we borrowed it to practice, but it's not there now."

"It's over here. Someone moved it to get it out of the way. Happy racing." And with that, he disappeared.

"Okay, ladies," from our coxswain, Fran. "Let's get a move on."

The eight of us awkwardly and uncomfortably squat into position under this rack built for munchkins.

"Lay hold, and up. Step it out. Walk it overhead out of the house."

When at the dock, "Toe to the edge and roll it in."

As we busily affixed our oars, there was chatter. Women laughed. They commented on who in their family was there to cheer us on, added disparaging remarks on the condition of the boat, and griped about having competition.

"Looks like this puppy hasn't been rowed since Nixon was in office."

"I don't think scholastic rowers ever row octopods. I'm amazed they keep one rigged for sculling."

"Given the condition of this boat, I'd say they never thought it was worth rigging it as an eight to use. Too old and decrepit."

"Port oars out, one foot in and down."

"Count down when ready."

And with that, we are stroking our way up the lake to the start.

"You're looking good, ladies," says our cox. "Nice and steady rate on the way up. Don't tire yourself out. Save it for the race."

At the start, we were quite a picture—us in our ragged excuse for a boat rowed by eight unmatched old ladies, and our competition, all in their club's rowing unis with matching visors. They were young and tanned, and their boat looked brand-new. The crew and the boat glimmered. On the other hand, we resembled an old, waterlogged tree limb having been tossed about for a bit.

"Oh, shit, whose idea was this? Look at that crew. They are serious racers," states Linda.

"And they are, what, average age thirty. What's our average age, sixty?" I ask.

"We should get a handicap because of the age difference," says Ann.

"A fifteen-second handicap will not help us against that highly polished team," I murmur.

From the starting referee, "Cleveland Heights rowing club in lane three. Wilmington rowing center in lane four.

"Attention," shouts the starter.

Our blades are squared in the water, and we are in the start position, arms outstretched, knees under the chin. And the gun is fired.

We are off half, half, three quarters, full stroke to pry us out of the water. These are swift, small strokes. I'm stroking a good forty-four (strokes a minute) to get us rolling. We followed up with fifteen-full power strokes to keep us moving. By now, I'm normally out of breath and energy. But today I don't notice because I'm exhilarated! We are racing!

"Oh my god, oh my god, my seat. I've come off the seat," I scream. This happens when a rower is overly enthusiastic and pushes so hard with their legs that their derriere flies off the seat. Most of the time, the seat comes below said derriere, but "Shit, where's my seat?"

"Your seat is off the rails," Ann yells behind me. "Can you continue to stroke?"

"No, I can't get a full stroke because I can't move back and forth; you have to take over stroke. Damn." And with that, I lay my blades flat on the surface, depriving our boat of one-eighth of its full power.

Down the line of eight rowers, women gasp, "What's going on? It looks like stroke is not rowing."

"Don't know, but Fran has not told us to stop. Keep rowing."

Lakeside, Lou and Linda's husbands are watching. Dan, Lou's husband, is cheering us on, but Pat, Linda's husband, is saying, "Um, something's not right."

We finished, but as you can imagine, we were far behind the young, shiny crew. We didn't even warrant a second-place medal because the octopod race was added after ordering trophies and metals. Bummer!

Fortunately, it was the end of the day, so most rowers and spectators had left the premises. No one from our rowing center ever said a word about our pitiful race. A group of men and women in our club got to rig an eight for sculling, and they raced Cleveland Heights and won. We were delighted for our club's rowers to show up the team who shamelessly beat some old ladies whose stroke lost her seat rowing an old crotchety boat.

CHAPTER 28

Ringing the Buoy

The maples are ablaze in the 9:00 a.m. light, brilliantly declaring it fall and nearing the end of our rowing season. But for now, we can enjoy this delicious show of red, gold, and green gracing the river's shores before pondering the bleak winter months without being on the water.

Fall is special on our river, not just for the eye candy, although that would be enough, but also for the crisp, cool fall air. Just breathing is a delight. By now, we have many rows under our belts, and our technique is the best of the season. We don't have to work as hard or concentrate as consistently. Our muscles have the memory of what to do and when to do it without any conscious effort on our part. Our bodies are aerobically fit and strong from hours of rows. This all leaves us free to enjoy the sensuous day.

The nonhuman species are less busy in the fall. Ducklings have left their mothers' feathered breasts, osprey fledglings have flown to claim their own territory, and turtles are not as evident since sun puddles are not as warm in the fall. It's quiet. Soothing.

The Panthers rowed upriver amidst this lovely spectacle. The tide was going out, so we were rowing against it.

"This is like rowing through butter," Linda shouted.

Ann responded, "Current is really strong this morning."

"You know, last night was a full moon. The tides get stronger when the moon is full," I added.

"Did it also rain last night? That could be adding to the current," says Linda.

"Ann, look—cormorants on the pier drying their wings!" I shout back.

"Where?"

"Two o'clock."

"What are you two saying?" Linda asks.

"Looking at the cormorants lining up on the pier drying their wings at two o'clock," Ann answers.

Lou is bowing and sometimes has trouble hearing what's going on upfront.

"Where do you see pomegranates? I didn't think they grew around here," she shouts.

Linda, laughing, "No Lou, cormorants, the birds."

Lou, now laughing with her, "Oh, I thought you were saying pomegranates."

Ann asks, "Linda, what is funny back there?"

Laughing, Linda tries to tell Ann what Lou has misheard. "Lou thought we said pomegranates."

Ann, "Pomegranates don't even grow around here. Where did she think she saw pomegranates?"

"What is Lou saying back there?" I ask.

By the time the messages of misheard words go back and forth and back again, the entire quad is in a laugh uproar.

"Ha, ha, ha, ha, ha, ha," Linda says, beside herself while Lou tries to explain how she thought she heard "pomegranates."

This is how we earned the name Quadraphonics, as the club president christened us. We are often heard laughing on the river.

"Okay, ladies, let's do a power ten to warm up these muscles," said Linda. "In two. One, two, and on for ten."

We did our power ten, twenty, and thirty pyramid, some steady state, some balance exercises, and slow-to-high stroke rate routines. We then rested at the neck of the port before turning to go back upriver.

"Has anyone here rung the bell?" I asked.

"You mean out in the Delaware?" asks Linda.

"Yeah, it's so calm today. It would be a good day for it. What do you say? Want to give it a try?"

"Danielle, how do you ring the bell? I mean, do you have to get out of the boat and stand on the buoy? I'm not sure I'm up for that," says Lou.

"I know a few from our club who have done this. Have you, Danielle?" Linda asks.

"Yeah, I did it in my single a couple of years ago."

"How far is the buoy into the main river?" asks Ann.

"It's just right at the mouth of the port. Not far out," I respond.

"Who would get out of the boat to stand on the buoy to ring the bell? Wouldn't the boat go over?" Lou asks.

I laugh, "Ringing the bell does not mean rowers getting out of the boat to ring the buoy bell. It means rowing a ring around the bell."

"Oh, that makes me feel much better," sighs Lou. "But I'm still not sure I like going to the port."

"Oh, come on. There's nothing to be afraid of. The tide is coming in, so we can't drift out to sea," I insist. "How does everyone else feel?"

"I'm good," says Linda.

"Okay by me," says Ann.

"All right. If that's what everyone wants to do," sighs Lou, sounding less than enthusiastic.

I have done this before in my single, but I pushed to do it in our quad. It was exhilarating. It made up for all the pranks I never did when I was young, all the fun things all the other kids told me about, like the daring things even my dad did when he was a kid. He told me that he and his pals would gather armfuls of fall leaves and throw them into any cars parked on the street with open windows. In the winter, they would climb onto the snow-covered garage roof and slide off into the snow piles (he was raised in Buffalo, so there was always an abundance of snow in the winter). He'd laugh when he mentioned they would occasionally tear off a gutter.

This fun escapade wouldn't create any cleanup, wasn't terribly dangerous, and wouldn't cause any damage to any property. Best of all, my mother wasn't around to tell me I couldn't do this because it wasn't ladylike, or she didn't want me hanging around whatever hooligans she thought I was playing with, or it just wasn't something a proper English girl should do. Well, Mom, I'm going for it!

So out we go. It is calm and beautiful, and the sun is shining. There are no container boats in the harbor; the sky is blue, no cumulous clouds, but it's still a little scary being out there. A ship could come up to the port entrance at any moment, and our quad doesn't have the horsepower to get out of the way with alacrity. Not only would we be in immediate trouble, but we would probably be thrown in jail. It's illegal for vessels other than container ships to be out here.

As we get close, Lou says, "What do we do now? Just go around it? Which way should we go? Clockwise, counterclockwise? Does it matter?" It's clear that Lou is getting very nervous.

Of course Linda is on her phone, talking to her husband. "Yeah, Hon, we are at the port just circling the buoy." She laughs. "We are fine. No cargo ships are in the port or anywhere we can see on the Delaware. Okay, we won't be here long." And to us, "Pat's afraid he will have to bail us out of jail." She laughs a halfhearted laugh. She's getting nervous out here.

Lou is next. "Dan, I just want to let you know we are at the mouth of the port where the buoy is. No, we are not in trouble; well, it's kind of like a rite of passage for rowers. If you come out here to ring the bell, you are accepted into the in crowd. I don't know which crowd, and I don't know why we are here. No, we don't ring the bell on the buoy; we row a ring around the buoy. Anyway, in case we don't make it out alive, I wanted you to know where to find the bodies." She turns to us, saying, "Dan says being out here is not good."

While I can hear the nervousness caused by this adventure, I also see the crew's pride. Now we can all brag about having "rung the bell." Yeah, that and five bucks might get us a cappuccino.

CHAPTER 29

Stuck in the Mud

Another balmy Sunday morning is a week later. "Lou, would you like me to bow today? You are always stuck back there. I want to give you a break so you can get a better workout."

Bow is so busy ensuring the quad stays on a course free of debris that she can't get a good workout. Our river winds around, making it necessary to check behind every minute. And because it's tidal, it pulls stuff off the shores at high tide and carries them out to the Delaware. Debris can include large trees that cleverly stick to the muddy bottom and wait for an inattentive sculler to come along and slash a big slice in their hull.

Some mornings after storms, we will have an entire debris field stretch from shore to shore, just waiting to gobble up whatever rows into it. The true dilemma with these mishaps is if a boat can't get free of one of these floating hazards, their number is up. They will float out to sea with the tree limbs, leaves, baby strollers, Styrofoam coolers, and dead vermin and be forever forgotten.

So the bow's job is serious and requires continuous alertness.

"Ya know, I will take you up on that, Danielle. Thanks. I don't want to take your stroke seat."

"I'll stroke, Lou," Ann says.

"Thanks, Ann."

"Beautiful morning. Weekends like this are soooo necessary," Ann says. "I need these days on the water to wash away the work politics."

During a break, "Have I ever taken you through the secret channel, ladies?"

"What secret channel?" from Ann.

"The one to the left of the river, just after the bridge on our way back."

"You mean where the river kinda splits?" asks Linda.

"Yeah, a nice quiet branch goes off to the left and rejoins a short way later. It's quite lovely. I use it in my single because it's so quiet and peaceful. Everyone okay with going there on our way back?"

A round of "Sure. Okay. Fine."

We cross under the bridge, and I steer toward the mouth of this sweet slice of heaven. The river is at high tide, so it will be deep enough for us to traverse this small inlet.

"Oh nuts, I may have cut the corner close, but I think we are okay. Ann, lay your starboard oar flat against the side of the boat so it doesn't hit the muddy island."

Stroke does as I asked, but we stop dead anyway.

"Okay, everyone, sit tight. I think we just snagged a muddy piece of that island. Stroke, drop out, and everyone else, take one hard stroke, annnnd row." But the boat is slipping sideways toward the island's bank, and the stern is stuck on something.

"Let's try that again, but this time with our best power, sit at the finish, ready all, annnnd row!"

Nothing.

"Ann, can you tell what's going on up there? What is holding us back?"

"It just looks like the stern is somehow stuck in the mud. And this current is pushing the boat sideways into the island. I'm going to try to push off." She does, but, "That's not working. The blade sinks into the mud."

"Okay, everyone. Let's have Ann and Linda try to push off the island with their oars, and Lou, you and I will take some 100 percent pressure strokes. Ready and row."

Nothing. Nada. We are not moving one lousy centimeter.

"I can't believe this. What the hell," I'm mumbling. I never get stuck, always able to get out of a jam. Just a matter of persevering. This is hurting my pride and beginning to worry me.

Ann volunteers, "I can get out of the boat and try to pull it off the island."

"No, Ann, this current is too strong. You could slip under the boat or get smashed between it and the island," I tell her.

"I could try to push it out if I get out on the port side. I can't get crushed there," offers Linda.

"No, with our luck, you'd get sucked around the bow and be pulled downstream. That's not going to work. No one is getting out of the boat. Too dangerous in this current," I'm shouting.

We tried the same maneuvers again, which didn't work the first time and didn't work again the second or third time. I'm pushing at the island, the muddy bottom, taking hard strokes, and accomplishing nothing. I can't believe we are this relentlessly stuck.

"You know, I think the tide is going out. The longer we are here, the more stuck we get. You know what I mean?" Ann observes.

"Great," says Linda, who has gotten out her cellphone, which is always at the ready. "No one at the boathouse is answering the phone."

"How would they get us out of this mud thing anyway?" Lou asks.

"Hi, Hon. We are stranded on the Christina, and I don't know how long we will be here. We seem to be stuck in the mud. No, you can't help. We'll figure it out. Just wanted to let you know," Linda warned her husband.

Everyone then calls someone to tell them of our fix. Lou's husband says, "That doesn't sound good." Linda's husband says, "Stay safe and keep me informed. If you want me to try to find you, I will." My husband, however, is laughing his fool head off. "How the hell did you do that?" he asks. He must have more faith in our ability to escape this mess than I do now. On the other hand, he finds humor in the most bizarre aspects of life; in his view, most of life is bizarre.

"Okay, ladies, I'm calling 911," declares Linda.

Within five minutes, a helicopter was circling over us.

"Oh no, they are filming us. Will we be on the 6 o'clock news?" cries Linda. "The entire boathouse will know." If Lauren had been in this boat, she would have said, "Girls, look up, smile pretty, and do the queenly wave!" We could have used her humor about now.

We felt like beached fish at low tide, flopping about, losing steam, and running out of big ideas. One sign of a true sculler is getting themselves out of any jam. We couldn't manage this and would never live it down at the boat club.

"I hear a motorboat. They're coming," says Lou. A fire rescue boat comes toward us, asking if everyone is okay. They soon realize that the tide is too low for them to get close to us. They consult the big bosses on their radios.

"They are sending a flat bottom boat. He'll be able to get close enough to get you out." Great, now our humiliation is tripled. First, the helicopter had to scope us out, then a big boat couldn't maneuver close enough, and now we warrant a third rescue attempt. Could it get any more humiliating? I guess the Coast Guard and city police could get involved. Or maybe the scuba division of the National Guard could show up with their bells, whistles, and more helicopters and drones taking pictures.

Shortly after, a fireman dressed in fatigues, clearly ready for serious duty, arrives in a gray flat-bottomed raft not unlike what whitewater rafters use. He tries to step onto the island and slides through the mud smack dab up to his hip in water. Not exactly an awe-inspiring move. Back in his raft, he says, "Here's what we are going to do. You will hand me your oars, one by one, and then step out of the boat into this raft."

"No, no," I'm yelling. "We will go over if we take the oars out of the water."

"No, you won't. I've got hold of you."

"You don't understand. This boat has no keel. It has an entirely round bottom. It will go over." Now I'm beginning to panic that we will all go into the river, or he will break this boat in half by hanging onto it, and we will all go into debt to pay for it. "It's also made of a delicate material and doesn't do well with stress along its length. It could break right in half." I'm really shouting now. I am terrified.

"It will be fine," he says. "Trust me. Come on now. You first," he says to Ann. She undoes her oars from the oarlocks, hands them to him, and, with his steady arm, walks off the side of the scull into his raft. From there, she boards the larger boat.

This process is repeated three more times until we are all safely aboard the fire rescue boat. He was right. The boat was in one piece, and so were we. The ride to the boathouse was quiet except for my crew, who noticed the Basset hound hangdog look on my face and told me, "It wasn't your fault."

If it had been a man's boat, the rest of the crew would have said, "What the hell did you think you were doing? Didn't you see the island there? Where did you learn to bow?"

Women are always kind and forgiving.

And later, as expected, we were ridiculed at the boathouse. One bitchy female stated at a board meeting, "There is no excuse for having to be rescued. If I had to swim the entire length of our river back to the boathouse dragging the boat, I would have opted for that over being rescued."

It made me wonder if she had been taking doses of testosterone or had an undisclosed Y chromosome hidden in her DNA.

CHAPTER 30

Are We Talking
About Rowing or Sex?

Out on the water, the Panthers warm up per instructions from Lou. I'm stroking and Ann is behind me with Linda in two seat. It's been months since the accident on the river, and we have been rowing enough to regain our confidence completely. But every time we row upriver, we glance at the Cobra. It's still there; sometimes, when the tide is low, we can see it just breaking the surface. It now has a bright orange cone to keep other boats from hitting it.

"So what do you want to do today?" asks Lou. We can do steady state up and a workout on the way back or whatever you want. What do you think?"

"We should work on our racing starts at some point," I say. We plan on racing in the Diamond States Regatta, which is a month and a half away.

"How about we do a power pyramid on the way up and I will call some technique things to work on as we row," says Ann.

"Great," says Lou. "Linda, do you want to call the power?"

"Sure, let me know when we have a clear straightaway, Lou."

It's not usual that anyone besides the bow in a quad calls commands, but our crew has learned to share the workouts that way. Linda sits right in front of Lou and calls out whatever workout we agree on for the rows. She checks with Lou to be sure we are not coming up on a bridge or any other congestion before she starts the piece. We joke that Linda is the only one in our boat who can reliably count strokes.

"Okay to go, Linda," says Lou. Lou's commands are always gentle. She's full of thank-yous and pleases when she needs our help turning, slowing down, speeding up, or whatever. And she has one of those voices that can be so lyrical that sometimes her commands sound like tiny bird songs.

"In two, power ten. That's one, two, here we go for ten," says Linda, and we are pushing at 90 percent for ten strokes.

After ten power strokes, we paddle for ten to catch our breath.

And then, "In two, power for twenty, that's one, that's two, and here we go for twenty," says Linda.

"The next ten are for clean catches," yells Ann. Ann has more experience racing than the rest of us, and so we rely on her to monitor our technique.

At the end of our workout, Linda shouts, "In two, let it run!"

"Wow, that was great," says Lou.

"Whew, yeah," says Ann.

I cannot say a word since I cannot breathe.

"We must work on long, strong strokes during the power pushes," says Ann.

"Said the actress to the bishop," I respond still gasping for breath.

Laughing, Linda says, "That's so funny."

"Yes," Ann pipes in, "we need to keep the recovery slow, slow, slow, and the drive strong and hard."

"After we've done our fast and strong fifteen high at the start," adds Lou, screaming with laughter.

"And remember to concentrate on quick hands away," chimes in Linda, referring, of course, to the need to prepare quickly for the next stroke.

"Make sure we have clean and crisp finishes," I say.

"Curl your toes and pull up," squeaks Lou.

"Hold the orange between your knees," croaks Linda—a friendly reminder to keep our knees together and not let them splay.

"Remember not to go too deep on the strokes," I add.

"Pull hard on port," laughs Linda, hardly able to get it out.

"Nice smoooooth layback," says Ann.

"Finish with a hard-driving power twenty and let it run," adds Lou.

By now, we can hardly keep the boat steady; we are laughing so hard. I don't know if rowing terms are purposefully sexual or if we are bending them to seem so, but this is not the first time we have discovered the similarity. For some reason, each time we do, it seems as though we are freshly discovering this delight.

Ann rowed with an all-male crew once who, she said, disgusted her with comments about flatulence and prostrate problems. She shriveled her nose at the discussion and probably the odors and was asked sarcastically, "Well, what do women crews talk about?"

"Sex," Ann responded and smiled with her I'm-single-and-sexy smile.

CHAPTER 31

When There Is
Ice on the River

Rowing season invariably ends in our neck of the woods by October. Linda spends the winter with her grandkids or at her condo in Florida, Ann hits the pool at the Jewish Center, and Lou and I are always a bit adrift for some winter sports. One winter, we met three times a week to do Zumba on a CD we had purchased. But the routine got boring.

Another year, we found a weight-training class on YouTube; this had the added benefit of working out at home. The coach's voice was singsong irritating, and we ran into technical difficulties. We would dial up the YouTube videos on our computers or iPads and then FaceTime over the phone. When it worked, it worked great. We could do the same workout simultaneously and hear each other complain about how tough it was via FaceTime. The problem is that often it didn't work. One or the other of us would have Internet difficulties, and we would chat for an hour.

One year, at one of our last rows, I suggested quad roller-skating during a discussion about what sport we could do over the winter. Lou agreed that sounded great, and we both went our separate ways. Within a few days, she had a pair of skates she found on the Facebook marketplace and was ready to rock and roll. I was stunned. It was a throwaway idea. Good lord, I hadn't skated since I was fourteen! And that's not counting the rollerblading disaster.

But Lou was already well into the idea. She had the skates, the protective gear, and visions of doing Motown moves on the sidewalks. So I got some decent sky-blue Barbie doll skates, and we looked for an excellent space to begin.

We tried a shopping mall parking lot first. Gleefully donned our skates, knee, elbow pads, helmets, and wrist pads and tried to stand up. Even that proved more challenging than we expected. After a few tries and getting very discouraged, Lou invented training wheels. She went up and down her driveway using her dad's rolling walker. She took videos to convince me that it was safe and that we could stay upright.

We found a brand-new colossal parking lot at the university: no concrete cracks, acorns, or twigs. We thought we were in business. But staying upright still eluded us. As long as we hung onto George as Lou christened her dad's walker, we were okay, but if we dared let go we were in trouble.

Lou scoped out a tennis court for us to try, thinking the surface might be smoother and softer. I agreed to try because I fancied the falls would hurt less on the more forgiving surface. However, the court, which had signs saying, "No use other than tennis," was near enough to trees to be festooned with acorns and twigs. Even tree leaves at this point in our "practice" would take me down. And no matter how soft the surface, a bad fall hurt. My muttered mantra of "I did this at fourteen, for god's sake; how can it be so much harder at seventy?" didn't help. I was ready to give up.

But the Energizer Bunny was not about to give up. "I found an indoor rink not too far away, and they give lessons. Maybe they could teach us the Motown dance moves." (After seeing some cool videos, this had become our goal.) Okay, so I was ready to try one more time.

This meant that we now needed to buy indoor wheels and some decent ball bearings. This was more investment in something that had me doubting. We showed up with our skates, protective gear, credit cards, and enthusiasm.

We met our instructors, Stephanie, Thumper, and Reid. God knows what they must have thought seeing a sixty-something and seventy-year-old show up for beginner lessons.

We took lessons every Saturday morning all that first winter and managed to stay upright most of the time. As the instructors got to know us and realized we wouldn't quit at the first tumble, they even invited us to practice at the rink on nights when they taught private lessons. They also introduced us to the Tuesday/Thursday morning coffee skate, which we would occasionally attend if Lou had a day off.

It took Lou and I a couple of skating seasons to realize that Motown was off the agenda. These instructors all practiced and taught artistic skating. This was not exactly what we set out to do, but they became so dear to us during our winter weekends that we strived to learn those postures, moves, and finally, tango, waltzes, and foxtrots.

During those five years, I was the one who fell all the time. Risk-averse I am not! I would try just about anything. Lou, on the other hand, was a cautious Nelly. She even found some hip- and butt-padded pants, which she called her "pants of courage." Neither of us ever really injured ourselves too severely. Maybe my pride was hurt occasionally, watching the instructors make a beeline to me each time I fell to ensure I was all right. I guess they did not want to be liable for a seventy-year-old's broken bone or head.

Lou's technique was always spot on: knees bent, torso straight, and arms holding a "Cinderella skirt," as we had been taught to think of our body placement. Thumper had descriptions to help us visualize stances and moves. She would tell us "Follow your boobs around on the turn" or "hoist your right cheek up when you kick back."

When I would tire of perfecting the dance steps, figure eights, and skating backward and turns, I would skate around the rink fast, creating a slight breeze and enjoying the glorious, carefree freedom. Thumper would break the reverie at these moments by yelling from across the rink, "No Betty White." Apparently, in my delirium, I would be swinging my arms like a butterfly enjoying the flight. Thumper likened my freestyle to the typical dumb blonde roles Betty White so often played. It was not precisely the artistic skating she was trying to teach us.

Reid was often used to demonstrate the moves Thumper or Stephanie were teaching to the class. Reid had only been skating there for about six years when we started lessons. He was tall and thin and looked so polished and graceful at thirty-something that you'd think he had been skating all his life. As the years went by, Reid taught some beginner classes and always coached us when free.

Sometimes we would ponder our handsome, winsome Reid's situation, living with his parents and "loveless." Lou and I would talk about who we might fix him up with. He once told us, "I started skating to meet women only to discover all women here are over seventy." Then he would laugh. He found community at the rink, becoming besties with Stephanie and establishing acquaintances like me and Lou. He was easy to be around—always smiling, teasing, or joking and quick with a laugh. We grew to adore him. He was the icing on the skate cake!

At one point, Lou invited her husband and daughter to watch us practice. Watching figure skaters, dance skaters, and speed skaters can be lovely and exciting, but watching two old ladies trying to stay upright on their skates for an hour, well, not so much.

Our rowing friends thought we were crazy taking up skating. Time and time again, we would ask one of the others if they wanted to join us. Invariably, the response was, "Are you crazy?" Fear of getting hurt was the thwarting factor here. All I could think was, damn, if fearing hurt and pain keep you from trying new things, then how do you keep life exciting?

And then, one day at seventy-five, I went to the first class of the fall season. Something had changed. I couldn't do the figure eights I had so gracefully perfected in prior years. Even one curve was evading me. I tried a few more weeks to get to that comfortable spot with these moves, only to aggravate a hip. I was puzzled, bewildered, and, most of all, angry. What the heck was going on?

At seventy-five, my body was telling me, "Enough already." Arthritis had set in, and despite my strength training, rowing, and Zumba, this malady was going to have its way with me. I could still skate, but the turns, crossovers, and figure eights eluded me. I wasn't finished yet. I had not learned all that I set out to learn. I was nowhere near wanting to give up.

Maybe, after Lou retires, we will go to Tuesday/Thursday morning coffee skate with the other old folks. But for now, it was sayonara to my newfound, short-lived endeavor. I miss the challenge, spending time with my friend Lou, and working with my super funny teacher friends Stephanie, Thumper, and Reid. Those three have become a lovely, if short-term, addition to my life.

CHAPTER 32

Teacups and Ferris Wheel

"Hey," Ann emailed in October, after the season's end, "I have a friend I work with at the hospital who has offered me her place at Ocean City for the weekend. It has two bedrooms and four beds. What do you think, ladies? Shall we go? I could sure use a girls' weekend!"

"Great idea. I'm in," I reply.

"Me too," from Lou.

"I grew up going to Ocean City. I love it there. I think my cousin goes every weekend. They have a place there. I'm in," says Linda, who I'm convinced has cousins in every borough, town, county, and state.

So, we agreed to meet there on Friday afternoon.

"I'll bring breakfast omelet stuff," from Ann.

"I can do a vegetable soup for supper for Friday night," chimes Linda.

"I can bring wine, Prosecco, and snacks," adds Lou.

"I'll bring weed and some fizzy drink. I think I have a recipe for peach daiquiris or something."

"I'll send everyone directions once you get to Ocean City. This will be fun."

On that Friday afternoon, I'm on the phone. "Hey Linda, I'm lost. I can't find the street or see any of the landmarks Ann mentioned."

"It's Danielle, she's lost," Linda says to Ann and Lou next to her. "Have you followed route 1 to . . ." This conversation continued with questions.

"I got to Ocean City but can't find the street."

"Let me have the phone," from Ann. "Okay, do you see . . ." and we continue to figure out where I am and how to get where I'm supposed to be.

Finally, Linda pipes in, "She sees what?" and begins to laugh. "Oh my god, she's in Ocean City, Maryland."

"Yeah. Where the heck am I supposed to be?

There is a chorus of three on the other end of the line. I can hear them giggling, but trying to control their laughter so they don't hurt my feelings. "We are in Ocean City, New Jersey, Danielle," says Ann.

"There's an Ocean City, New Jersey?" There was more laughter from Ocean City, New Jersey. "I didn't know that!"

I always went to the Maryland beaches. Who would've guessed there were two Ocean Cities? As I drove from my Ocean City to that other Ocean City, I wondered who named these places, and why on earth anyone would name two places an hour away from each other "Ocean City" defies logic. I decided then and there that I had missed my calling. I should have been a city namer. I'm smart enough not to do something so stupid.

An hour later I arrive. Soup is warming, and I bring out the fizzy drink concoction, some vodka and tonic, and "roses." This group often communicates by email and text and has renamed marijuana "roses." I guess since it's still illegal, they fear getting thrown in jail. I can't imagine any judge wanting to throw four old ladies in prison for smoking pot, but I go along with their wishes. Roses it is.

Everything is funny after the soup, great bread, fizzy drinks, and roses. Lou keeps telling us she's not high and heads to the kitchen for another hit. "Are you high?" she asks Ann, sitting beside her. Ann laughs, "Yes, and so are you."

"I'm not feeling it," says Lou. Three minutes later, "DJ [what she calls me], are you high?"

"Yes, Lou, and so are you." She tosses another handful of chips into her mouth and heads to the kitchen again, mumbling, "I don't feel it."

Maybe ten minutes later, "Ann, are you high?"

We are hysterical watching her being high and not realizing it.

Linda is, of course, on the phone with her cousin, arranging to meet her somewhere tomorrow. The rest of us find this hilarious as Linda is the most social person. Once at a restaurant with our spouses for dinner, she was interrupted three times to get up from our table to say hello to people she knew. I can't take her anywhere! Someday we will probably find Linda has cousins on Mars.

Meanwhile, Lou, who swears she isn't high, begins to talk gibberish. "Annie, can you talk with your hands like this?" She has made squirrel paws of her little hands and is poking Ann on the arm with them. "Tse, tse, tse" she is muttering.

"Don't make me laugh; I have to pee," I shout, making a beeline for the bathroom. Linda, who doesn't smoke this stuff and barely drinks, is bent over laughing and falls to the floor at Lou's antics. Ann is calmly shaking her head.

When I return, Lou has scuttled her legs and feet under the sofa cushion and is leaning against the sofa arm. She has her eyes closed and is softly snoring.

We have finished the fizzy drinks, the snacks, and the last of the tequila. I, for one, am having trouble standing and wondering how I will navigate the stairs.

"Lou, time to go to bed," says Ann.

"I'm here. I'm fine."

"No, come on, Lou, let's get you to bed."

"I'm perfectly comfortable here," she says. "You all go ahead." And with that, she goes back to snoring. She had slipped under both sofa cushions, so Linda put a pillow under her head, and we headed for bed.

I woke up the following day to the glorious smell of coffee and omelet. Ann was cooking. Surprisingly, we all felt pretty good.

Reading a local paper left on a side table, I say, "There's a movie theater in town. *Purple Rain* is showing. Want to go? Show time is 11:00."

"Sure, what the heck. That sounds good. We can make it," says Linda. "I promised my cousin I'd meet her sometime while we were here. Would you mind if she joined us for dinner tonight?"

We want this weekend to be for just us. "Okay, we can meet her where you want to get takeout, but can we make it just us for dinner?" I ask.

"Okay, I'll let her know. She can also meet us on the beach tomorrow morning." Here she goes again. Our social butterfly. It's not like she hasn't seen or talked to her cousin in a long time. She lives two miles away, and they probably spoke a week ago.

The movie theater is one of those old theaters. Velvet drapes instead of doors close off the concessions from the theater entrance, and there are many tassels and ropes. We are the only ones in the theater. It's a kick.

We are walking the boardwalk back to the house after the movie. "Wow," cries Lou," an amusement park!"

"Let's get some tickets and check out the rides," I suggest. Lou is in immediately. Ann has decided to pick up some sandwiches, walk back to the house, and then go to the beach.

"What do we want to ride on first?" I ask.

"I don't know, ladies. I'm afraid of the Ferris wheel."

"Afraid of the Ferris wheel?" I ask in disbelief. "Why?" I always think of the Ferris wheel as tame compared to other rides.

"I just always have been."

"Well, we can fix that," I tell her. "We can start doing bumper cars and get you on the Ferris wheel. No worries."

"So where is everybody?" I ask the kid at the gate to the bumper cars.

"Not too many people are around in October," he says. "I'll come in with you. It's more fun when more cars are going."

"Great," I say. Linda says she isn't interested in bumper cars, so Lou, the "kid," and I head into our cars. We bang into each other, oversteer, and bang into the walls, then ricochet off those and run into the tires in the middle. It is more fun with more cars. It is also more fun when you are fourteen and your date is purposely and continually banging your car, eliciting your giggly fourteen-year-old female complaint.

"Okay, Linda, time's up, "I tell her as we head to the Ferris wheel. "We are here with you, and nothing is going to happen. You don't have to look down. Just out to the beautiful ocean."

"Okay," she hesitantly replies. We load her and ourselves into the small car and continue to reassure her. It's not a giant wheel, but if vertigo is your issue, anything over the height of a twenty-year-old azalea bush might as well be the Empire State Building.

She seems to be doing okay as we head up to the top. Lou and I are intent on distracting her with conversation until we reach the top. We can now see the ocean, and the view is beautiful.

"You were right; this isn't too bad," says Linda. Then there's a jerk and a halt as the car swings just a bit. Uh-oh.

"What's that?" Linda gasps, turning pale. "Why have we stopped? What's wrong? Are they going to leave us here?" She is panicking.

I'm sure she has visions of firetrucks and rescue ladders and frets that she might have to climb down a ladder. Looking down, I realize the kid is just stopping the wheel long enough to load another couple into a car. Thank God.

"It's okay; Linda, he's just loading some people into another car. We will be moving in a minute," I tell her. She's growing whiter but trusts us, and Lou holds her hand. We are moving again in a few minutes—a great sigh of relief from all three of us. I wasn't relishing the ladder descent either. Why did these things not even cross our minds when we were kids?

Linda can't wait to get her feet on firm ground again when we reach the bottom. "That wasn't as bad as I thought it would be." Her face didn't pink up, however, for another five minutes.

"What shall we do next?" Lou asks.

Linda immediately pipes up with, "Oh, the teacups. I love the teacups."

So over we trek to the teacups. Many of you know what this ride is, but for those who don't know, let me introduce you. Each "car" you sit in looks like a teacup, okay? Sounds innocuous, right? Each of these cups holds maybe six people at most, and in the center of the cup is a steering wheel sitting parallel to the floor. This is the wheel everybody hangs onto so they don't get thrown around. That's the theory.

The ride begins to spin the cup slowly and is quite pleasant. But soon, gremlins below the teacup get to work maliciously, increasing the spin rate. Participants jam into each other, first to the right and then quickly back to the left. The wheel, also operated by these sadistic gremlins, mysteriously rotates faster, leaving you grappling for purchase to right yourself. As you get used to these developments, the cup traverses around the circular ride, going up and down mounds. At that moment, you are faced with side-to-side jerking and banging, up-and-down floating, and uncontrolled spinning. I'm convinced these gremlins get paid by the degree of bruising on passengers' bodies or the resemblance of the riders' cheeks to those of a dog hanging his head out the window of a car doing seventy.

"You are afraid of the Ferris wheel and love this thing?" I scream to Linda. "What's wrong with you? You are crazy."

Meanwhile, Linda is laughing her fool head off, enjoying the hell out of this crazy thing. "Isn't this a hoot?" she gasps.

"Hoot?" I say, "This is torture." I'm shouting through bumps forward into Linda, backward into Lou, forward again . . .

Lou is trying her damnedest to take a video of this experience, but she can't hold onto her phone as this thing is jerking her tiny body all over this teacup. She's also laughing uncontrollably.

When the beast finally stops, we are exhausted, probably from laughter but also from being unable to breathe. I rode this thing at a fair as a kid, but I don't remember it being so exhausting.

As we begin to walk and recover, Lou starts laughing again. "Here, look, it's my video. I dropped it at the beginning."

All we can see are our blurry laps. But the sounds are clear. I'm screeching at Linda, "How can you be afraid of Ferris wheels and love this tortuous thing?" Linda and Lou are laughing hysterically.

Every once in a while, Lou still sends pictures of the three of us at the top of the Ferris wheel and the ridiculous video of our teacup ride.

CHAPTER 33

Panthers Decide to Race

Never having been a racer, I can't testify to what compels adult rowers to compete. They no longer engage in school rivalry, aren't vying for the Olympic team, and can only steal a few hours a week away from careers and families in what I consider the middle of the night, at 5:00 a.m., to practice. Additionally, many hot, often muggy, summer Friday afternoons are spent driving trucks hauling trailers of long, skinny, delicate, precariously perched boats to one river or another to compete at weekend regattas.

And it's not as if substantial prestige is earned among one's community outside of the rowing venue by bragging about medal winning. Rowing is not a beloved American pastime, unlike football, basketball, baseball, or soccer. Indeed, more uninitiated are impressed by whitewater rafting, canoeing, or kayaking adventures than rowing accomplishments.

My notion of rowing left over from childhood was of a flat-bottomed, aluminum fishing boat Dad rowed from shore to cove, lagoon, or some secret special spot that fish coveted for hanging out early in the morning. In that rowboat, I learned to hold my breath, grab the slimy worm out of the coffee can, lace him onto the hook, tie a sinker onto my line, and drop the messy thing over the side of the boat.

Hour upon hour, we spent sitting in that rowboat without uttering a sound lest the fish hear us, making sure not to lean over the side where our shadow would alert them to our predatory presence or move around enough to create telltale ripples to alarm them. I naively believed that fish were that clever.

I was ten and loved being alone with my dad. But have you ever tried to keep a ten-year-old quiet for even an hour? My butt would slowly go to sleep on the hard aluminum seats. The only occupation while waiting for something to happen was watching my dad light cigarette after cigarette, dangle the butt in his mouth, and slowly pull the line on his rod slightly up and down to make the soggy worm appear alive to any not-quite-awake fish.

I was bored to tears at the passive, silent pursuit and quickly tired of holding my pole with the tantalizingly tasty nightcrawler camouflaging the nasty hook that we foolishly thought might convince that sixteen-pound wall-eyed bass to accept as our luncheon offering and thereby become our dinner.

For others, rowing conjures up Hollywood's 1950s version of a Viking ship powered across endless miles of the Pacific by hundreds of galley-enslaved people rowing in unison. In squalid conditions and with a burly, sweaty crewman pounding out the stroke rate, oarsmen suffered from hunger, thirst, and fatigue. Chained to their oars, they were often rendered unconscious until Charlton Heston or Kirk Douglas revived them from near death with fresh water and freed them from the chains that held them captive to their oars and their dreadful fate.

In high school, rowing crews are often comprised of the football, baseball, basketball, and soccer team rejects. It is not considered a mainstream sport, and indeed, in many cities, it cannot qualify for state funding because of the lack of interest. Scholarships for rowing are more plentiful than most people realize and almost a sure way for someone to get into college. But it does not have the panache of other sports. No cheerleading squads are assigned to regattas, and few rowing champions are hired as spokespersons for sports products.

The value of rowing changes with age. In high school, it's a great way for guys to meet petite young women who cox their crews and share their passion, but that is about all. Things get a bit more serious in college, and Olympic gold beckons in the way that skating and skiing do. And later in life, it is a sport that can be engaged in as a single rower or part of a team and provides serious competitive challenges in vast numbers of adult regattas, culminating in Nationals and Internationals and the coveted Henley Regatta on the Thames, where it all began.

Regattas are held all over the country on calm rivers, reservoirs, and lakes and are sponsored most often by the local clubs whose members practice on those waters. My club sponsors an annual regatta on a small lake that attracts about a thousand rowers for the event. Each year, it is a huge undertaking and requires many club rowing volunteers and several Boy and Girl Scout troops to pull off safely. It generates money for the purchase of new club equipment. And, even for those who row recreationally, our regatta beckons us to join in the fun just for the heck of it.

Each boat submits the ages of each rower, a nasty requirement for women over thirty, so that heats can be constructed based on the average age of the rowers in the boat. If there are not enough boats in a specific age group, some boats in heat will have their times adjusted to compensate for the diminished capability of their aging bodies. A paltry fifteen-second handicap is hardly sufficient to pay for the age difference between thirty and sixty.

Sprint races are usually one thousand meters. Medals and trophies are awarded based on time to complete the course. If a boat wins a heat, it does not necessarily mean the crew wins a trophy. A winner of another heat (in the same category) may finish the course with a faster time. Getting excited on the sidelines is challenging if you can't tell if the boat winning the heat will walk off with the medal. This is one of the elements of rowing competition that renders it less than a stellar spectator sport.

A rowing heat does not generate the irresistible crowd excitement and yells of "Come on, StinkyPete" from a crowd watching a dark horse gain the lead from five horses behind on a last-minute sprint to cross the finish line first and steal the victory from the nose of the favorite.

Nor does it create that moment of breathless silence and subsequent gasp from a packed stadium witnessing the finesse of an experienced pitcher reading the catcher's signal, affecting a slight nod of understanding, winding up for the big pitch, and unexpectedly whipping the ball to the second baseman with lightning speed to catch a runner off base.

Rowing lacks, too, the excitement of home team fans shouting, rallying, jumping out of their seats, and cheering as they do for football's three-hundred-pound mountains of muscle to bash into the other team's three-hundred-pound muscle mountains, break bones, and create concussions, all to move a small leather, stylishly pointed at both ends, ball a couple of feet.

It is more interesting to watch Olympic rowing competitions on TV. Cameras are fixed to drones above the boats to display a crew's progress. Still, other cameras catch the action from the water level as each team sees their competition. These cameras follow each race, giving the spectator an uninterrupted view of the entire race. And sometimes crews do come from behind to win unexpectedly.

But at a live regatta, spectators can't see the complete course. It's about as interesting as those long hours hanging a worm over the side of a boat waiting for that one stupid fish.

At one time in our club, a group of women made up what the club called the "women's racing team." That meant that three times each week, eight adult women rowed sweep for an hour or so with a coach who tried to place them into the correct seats for their talents and adjust their technique to create a winning team.

The women's racing team had been together for several years with no change in crew. Newcomers were welcome when someone physically relocated, experienced injury, or died. This crew was maintained as is, but not because they had a winning formula. Indeed, they had been losing regattas together and complaining about it for years. But they refused to chance losing their seats on the team by competing for it. Rowing on the women's racing team then had nothing to do with ability.

They were a bitchy bunch as well. Any little misdemeanor committed by any club member was fair game for their scourge. If another crew was using the oars they favored, harsh words ensued. They complained when their launch was delayed waiting on other boats in the queue. And no one dared to sign out a boat they might choose to row on their scheduled evening. The racing team always demanded the first choice of boats.

Their crew was not sacrosanct either. If one of the crew should make a mistake, another will be sure to point out the misdemeanor.

"We would have won that heat if Marge hadn't gone deep."

"That didn't help, but Fran was also doing that left-leaning thing again."

"By the way, did you notice Joanne's roots?"

"Yeah, what's up with that? Can't she afford a box of Loreal?"

"She's just lazy, is all. And have you noticed that she is getting fat?"

The cat claws are always fully extended.

As an alternative to embarking upon a regimen of Xanax to alleviate his increasing frustration, Coach Fred tried to breathe new life into this group by taking them out of the sweep boat and grouping them into twos and fours for double and quad sculling.

But alas, he ran into problems here as well. None of them wanted to be bothered to learn how to bow the boat, and each had her specific reason.

"I would bow, but I can't turn my head far enough to be sure we won't crash into something.

"Sure, I'd be glad to help the team, but bowing would make me so nervous that I wouldn't be able to row well."

"You can't expect me to do it, but Fran can. She teaches third grade and already has eyes in the back of her head."

And when excuses ran dry, "I'm not going to do it. Find someone else."

The scuttlebutt around the club was that the women's quads and doubles were doing no better competitively than the sweep boat before, and the team was complaining louder than ever. Women who joined the club and were interested in racing were discouraged, and the coach was losing interest in spending time with such a dysfunctional group.

Along came the Pink Panthers. Now, my quad had no interest in racing. We were recreational rowers. But we had an exceptional rowing chemistry together. And we enjoyed each other and laughed a lot. Two of the four of us were experts at bowing, and there were never any complaints if someone on the crew messed up. We simply found the humor in it. We loved the boat we rowed and were just a tiny bit shocked to learn a year after we'd been rowing the Predator that it was a mid-weight men's quad. It didn't matter to the Panthers. We liked it, and it seemed to like us.

During a row, "So, shall we race at Diamond States (our club's annual regatta)?" Lou asked.

"Sure, that would be fun," said Linda.

"I don't know," I said, "I'm not much for racing. I hate it. Maybe you could find someone else to stroke."

"Oh, come on," said Ann. It'll be fun. And we need to race as the Panthers—all of us, no subs."

"I've done two sweep races and an octopod in my rowing career, and all three times, we came in dead last," I said. "I'm not interested in killing myself, even for five minutes."

"We don't have to kill ourselves," said Lou. "We could just do it for the fun of it."

"We could see if Coach Fred would give us a few pointers," said Ann, "so we can do our best."

"All right," I said reluctantly, "if everyone else wants to, I'm in."

The Panthers had cast caution to the wind. Coach Fred was delighted that another crew was genuinely interested in improving, especially one that had a bona fide bow person. He eagerly agreed to coach us.

CHAPTER 34

Panthers Practice

Most crews begin a race by prying the boat out of the water with quick, short strokes.

The next part of the start usually is fifteen high strokes, meaning full strokes as mean and mad as the crew can. Then the crew settles into a sustainable, steady row. By this time, the boat is cooking.

During the race, the bow may call for some power or to increase the rate if she thinks her crew is falling behind. Toward the end, she will ask for the crew to sprint. That means the finish is in sight, this is your last shot, it's do-or-die time, and you must give it whatever you have left to get across the line first—second, or anything besides last.

This ordeal should only last five or six minutes and cover one thousand meters. Some work so hard during these five minutes that they vomit when they finish. We are ladies and would never do that. Or, more honestly, we would never overwork ourselves to that degree. We believe it should be a fun sport!

"Attention!" shouts Lou. That's the signal that we place our oars in the water, ready to start.

"Row!"

We do our start and the fifteen high and let it run.

"We hit forty-four strokes a minute!" I shout back through gasps for breath.

"What did she say?" asks Linda.

"She said we hit forty-four," answers Ann.

"Yahoo," says Lou. "We will wipe that women's racing team off the course!!!"

"We are gooooood," says Ann.

We are very proud of ourselves. We were, after all, just recreational rowers. We never sought each other out. We just fell in together like a clique of teenagers.

Through the years of surviving the Cobra incident, which left us stranded in the Christina with a prolonged and scary rescue; risking being crushed by a container ship or jail time for ringing the buoy; getting stuck in the mud and needing yet another rescue—we fancied ourselves invincible. We were the four musketeers brought together by fate, ready to face any adversity and triumph. Nothing could thwart or defeat us now. We were the Panthers! And full of ourselves.

It was June. We had been rowing three times a week since April. We had two sessions with the club's coach to see if he could help us with technique.

"You girls keep practicing, and you will challenge the women's racing team. I wouldn't be surprised if you beat them and have a damn good chance of medaling at the regatta," Fred told us.

"No," Linda responds. "You really think so?"

"Hey, you have more enthusiasm, and you look really good out there. Yeah, you have a better-than-good shot. Keep it up."

I am dumbfounded, and Ann grins from ear to ear. The rest of us start laughing.

"Do you think he means that?" says Lou when he is out of earshot.

"I told you we were better than the women's team," she says. "I told you." Ann had gone to a couple of women's racing team meetings early in the season, thinking she might want to row with them. She reported that they were highly dysfunctional and not fun at all.

The Panthers had stars in their eyes, and their eyes were on the gold. We began to notice the attention to our progress from the women's and men's racers in the club. Most of those who race don't give the non-racers the time of day, but we were getting the "hi, how are ya's" down at the boathouse.

"Hey, I was watching you out there," from the men's racing chair. "You guys look terrific. Looking forward to seeing what you can do at Diamond States."

One night at a social function, one of the men's team members said, "Hey, I hear you are in a quad that is doing well. I'm looking forward to seeing you at Diamond States. It really focuses your workouts when you prepare for a race, doesn't it?"

And then there were the times when the women's racing team had scheduled the boat right after our row and were on the dock waiting for us to return so they could go out. They stood, hands on hips, frowning or glancing at their watches.

The Panthers named this behavior "the silent ridicule" and thought it funny. "How can anyone enjoy rowing if they take it all so seriously?"

That night, we were careful to do a beautiful sprint right in front of the dock before coming in. We had them worried. Fred spread the word, and the racers talked about this really hot crew. US! We couldn't believe it. We thought it was funny, especially when we flubbed a practice start.

CHAPTER 35

The Big Kahuna

Race day arrived. We were primed. We had done everything we could to prepare for this race. We had several coaching sessions, worked hard, and practiced three times a week for months. We were hyped by the accolades we received from our club and ready to show the world that recreational crews could win races.

We all drove to the regatta separately very early in the morning. I had forced myself to do twenty minutes at home that morning on my rowing machine because some veteran racer told me it helped on race day. Later, I wondered if he said that to wear me out for the race. Having downed my coffee and yogurt, I headed out. I needed to stop for gas but had plenty of time. While my tank was filling, I went into the store to pick up another coffee, thinking it would calm my nerves. I knew better, but I bought it anyway. Back in the car, I was on my way.

I felt a tug and slammed on the brakes. OMG, did I run over something? As I flew out of the car, I fully expected to find someone's dead handbag dripping makeup and coins, a flattened bag of someone's sausage egg muffin, a can of soda, or, god forbid, a whining puppy. But it wasn't something I ran over. It was something I tried to run off with. I had forgotten to put the hose back on the gas pump. It was dangling like a dead snake from my gas tank, severed from the mother pump. Figuring someone from inside would come storming out to hand me a hefty bill for the repair or make a citizen's arrest until the cops could get there and cart me off to misdemeanor court, I furtively cased the area, leaving the door open in case a quick getaway was imminent.

No one emerged from the store. No other customers ran toward me, haranguing me for my stupidity or asking how I escaped the asylum. Feeling every bit the distracted idiot and yet stunned that I garnered nary a passing glance, I pulled the pump handle out of my tank, strode as nonchalantly as possible to the pump, and saw no identifiable means of reattachment. There's nothing to do but leave it on the ground near Mama and take off. Not knowing the protocol for such a mistake, I did not leave my name and contact information. It's not exactly a promising start to race day.

When I arrived, the Boy Scouts were in full regalia, directing cars to the parking area away from the boat trailers. I attempted to reason with the scoutmaster that I was an essential member of the hosting rowing club, had lots of stuff to unload, and needed to park in the VIP section, but that fib got me nowhere. I was directed to park a hefty distance from the action. Balancing my water bottle, sweatbands, change of clothes, and the ill-advised coffee, I began the search for my boat, oars, and crew. I found all of that in one place. We were all there—the second hurdle was behind me.

"Okay," says Lou. "The program says our race time is eleven, so we have plenty of time."

"I'm nervous," said Linda.

"We'll be fine. We've practiced. We're in sync, and we are strong," says Ann.

"I'm excited," said Lou.

I'm not crazy about the race itself; my comment is more like, "I just want it to be over with so we can relax." I don't tell them about my morning gas hose escapade. I couldn't stand the looks of "Didn't think you were that absent-minded."

"Let's have a look around," suggests Ann. "That will focus our minds on something else."

We check out the launch and finish docks. This year, someone had the brilliant idea to rent a mister at the finish dock. This regatta always happens in July and it is invariably hot and humid. Heat exhaustion is not out of the question. So the mister is a nice improvement. This regatta is for masters only. No schools or youth clubs compete here. That and the fact that it is staged on a lake, not a river, is a big draw for racers. Clubs are claiming their nice grassy areas and setting up tents and chairs for their racers and families to rest and eat when not on the water. It appears everyone this year has brought along their prized mutts, who are chasing each other around racers' legs to sniff other mutts' butts and doing the old puppy bow to get the fun going. There is an exciting festive vibe. All we need is a ferris wheel and the damn teracup ride.

Since this regatta is one we sponsor, we stopped to talk with lots of our members as we walked around the grounds. Everyone asks on race day, "Are you racing today?" Details of what, when, and with whom are exchanged, followed by "Good luck." We separate for these meanderings and meet up again at the vendors for the perusal of the latest rowing togs and jewelry. And one or the other of us gets into a conversation with someone, and we lose each other again.

Until "They just called our race," cries Ann as she rushes up to me.

"That's impossible," I say. "It's only 9:30. Our race is not till 11:00. Why would they call it now? Are you sure?"

"Yes, I'm sure. I checked with the launch captain after I heard the call. Where are Linda and Lou?"

"They were here a minute ago."

Ann and I run around until we gather our crew, frantically grab our oars, and carry our boat to the launch dock.

The dock master says, "You guys are late."

"So we hear, but the program said we weren't due to race till 11:00."

"Program? Didn't you check the board?"

"Board. What board? We looked at the published race schedule in the program," says Lou.

"That's not the final schedule," says the official sarcastically." The final schedule is posted on the board at the pavilion on the morning of the races. Haven't you guys raced before?"

"No," I murmur. And to the rest of the crew as we carry our boat to the water, "How are we supposed to know these things? Coach never told us. If there is a program that lists race times, you assume those are the race times. Is there a special course we were supposed to take on racing? What the heck?"

We get the quad in the water; Lou holds it for us as we hurry to get the oars to the dock.

"You guys were supposed to be here five minutes ago," says the assistant dock master. "Your competition is already heading to the start. I'll see if I can get the starter ref to hold for you, but you better hustle your butts on up there."

Now we are anxious, frustrated, angry, hassled, and harried. "Adjust your shoes on the water, ladies," suggests Lou. "That way, we can start up the course instead of staying docked until everyone is ready."

We get our oars in, and Lou says, "One foot in and down."

In the boat, Lou and Linda are beginning the row up to the start while Ann and I adjust our shoes. Ann and I row in a minute so the others can adjust theirs. Could we be more discombobulated by this point?

"I'm pissed," says Ann while fumbling her shoes.

"Me too," says Linda. "Just how are we supposed to know these secret race rules?"

Lou is now shouting at a launch boat blocking our path. "We need to get past you to get to the start. All the other boats in our race are up there. You have to get out of our way."

But the launch is not moving. They are trying to shout something back to us. I can only hear, "Wait till the last race goes by."

Lou is now screaming, "We have to get to the start. We are late. Just move the friggin' launch."

There was more shouting from the launch and more frantic yelling from Lou, who never swears. Finally, the launch moved, and we could get motoring to the start.

Lou is now mumbling, "What the heck was wrong with them? They were smack in our way, and I couldn't get past them. Ladies, we need to pick up the stroke rate to get up there in time."

We learned later that the lake narrows at that point, and with racers coming down the course and only sometimes known for staying in their lanes in their haste to win, there is potential for collision with boats traveling in the opposite direction heading to the start. If we had been on time, we would have been past this point before the prior race started.

We arrive at the start and maneuver ourselves to our starting position. Everyone else has been cooling their jets there waiting for us. They don't look pleased, and neither does the starting referee. But it doesn't matter. We made it. We are hyped. We are ready.

"Attention!" shouts the starter ref. All boats are in position with blades in the water, ready to push back and take that first stroke. Everyone is tense. Here's the moment we've been working toward all season. And the gun goes off.

At all regattas, there are referees. US Rowing trains these refs to take on specific responsibilities at all US Rowing–recognized regattas. There is a ref at the start who calls the race start, one at the finish who times each boat, and most others ride standing up in launches following the racers down the course. They stand in the boat with legs wide for balance, leaning back, hanging onto a rope affixed to the bow.

Their job is to watch all racers and ensure they follow the rules, stay in their lanes to prevent collisions caused by overenthusiasm, and to be available in the unlikely event of a rescue of racers ditched in the water. Since they control a crew's race, these refs can be full of themselves. They can call fouls if their version of rowers' behavior is judged inappropriate.

One year, another club's eight collided with one of ours during a race. The ref faulted the crew that T-boned our club's boat. Their coach tried to appeal the decision but was unsuccessful. Their coach further tried negotiating shared repairs of both boats with our club and was refused. The ref had named the T-boning club the offender, so they should pay for repairs to both boats. Such is the ref's absolute authority. I'm not clear on the details of who did pay for which repairs. Out of spite, the T-boning club boycotted our regatta for the next four years.

I understand the need for these officials; some are quite nice. Still, many of them remind me as they stand in these launches, legs spread, hanging onto a rope, leaning back with a smug look, of the masked Lone Ranger of '50s TV fame, who, at the end of the episode, as his white steed rears, is heard to shout, "Hi-yo, Silver, away!" And the townsfolk all utter, "Who was that masked man?"

We have an exemplary start. We are cooking, full of energy and pumped. We pry out of the water entirely in sync with quick-as-lightning half, half, three-quarter, full strokes. We are ahead of the boat next to us, and I'm feeling exceptionally stoked about our performance as we settle into our hard and fast high fifteen. All is going wonderfully.

Lou begins shouting, "The ref is waving a flag. I don't know what that means."

I see the flag he's waving from his exalted position in front of us, and I have no idea what he's trying to tell us, so I ignore him. I can't see where we are going and trust Lou implicitly. My job is to keep the stroke rate high and power strong.

"Just keep going, Lou," says Ann.

"But he's waving this flag. What does a white flag mean?"

"Ignore him," shouts Ann more vehemently.

We are going strong, neck and neck, with the boat next to us. I'm amazed at how adrenaline can wring more strength and endurance out of you. And especially if you are driving for something, you might win. I realize I'm beginning to enjoy this body-killing venture.

"He wants me to do something, but I don't know what. He's waving the flag at me. What should I do?"

To the ref, Lou shouts, "I don't know what you want me to do. What is the flag for? Does anyone know what that white flag means?"

And out of nowhere, someone shouts, "WAYNUF!" And we all stop rowing immediately.

Huh? What? What is happening? Who said that? Did a boat turn over? Are we going to crash into the survivors? Is there a tsunami coming, lightning, hailstorm, sea monster. Why are we stopping???? We were doing so well!

We stop as ordered, drifting idly, blades flat on the water. We are stunned. I watch our dream of finally winning dissolve as our competitors steal our glory, continuing the race. My heart is in my T.J. Maxx socks.

"Lou, what happened? Is there a boat behind us stopped?"

"Did someone crash into someone?"

"Are there rowers in the water?"

"No, ladies. Nothing has happened. The ref went right by us. I don't know why we stopped."

"I couldn't stand the shouting anymore. It was making me crazy. I just wanted it to stop," cried Ann. "From when the launch wouldn't let us pass to now, it's been shouting, shouting, shouting!"

She's correct, of course. It's been a bit of a Laurel and Hardy routine of who's on first with the race times being off, the frenzy of getting to the start on time, the pinch point thwarting our progress, and lastly, the Lone Ranger waving his white flag at us. We were all frazzled, but Lou was the most frazzled. As bow, she felt responsible for all of this.

"Well, ladies," says Lou. We have to finish rowing the course to get off the water. Sit at the finish and row."

Dreams crushed, hopes dashed. Oh well! We will never know if we could have bested our racing team. But this way, we could always believe we would have if that damn ref hadn't screwed us up with the white flag. The true irony was that that flag was meant for the crew beside us, who were creeping into our lane and in danger of crashing into us. The flag wasn't even for us.

No one in the boathouse said much except "What happened?" We just told them someone had caught a crab, and we had to stop. Winning wasn't ultimately important to us anyway. We were a wildcard. It somehow seemed fitting, given all the crazy adventures and mishaps we had had on the water, that this race would be no different. It would have spoiled our reputation if things had turned out differently. But alas, the gods conspired against us once again. No one blamed Lou or Ann for any of this. We were a team, and we shared responsibility. We had a good time and could live believing we might have won that race—if only.

Epilogue

Don't roll the credits just yet. The race was not the end of the Panthers by a long shot.

We rowed for many years after that race, enjoying our compatible style and continuing to perfect our technique and our friendships. It seems we had one race in us, and we had already used that one, but that differed from what we enjoyed about rowing anyway. Although we have each embarked upon new stages of our lives in other aspects, we rowed routinely until our bodies began screeching at us to trade the horse race for some sloth action. The backs complain, shoulders get overused, and hips and legs go wonky, making rowing increasingly uncomfortable.

Linda's family grew substantially to three grandchildren, and since they all live in Wilmington, Delaware, they are at Grandma's a lot. She watches the grandkids, feeds the clan, and hand-makes beautiful one-of-a-kind things for those babies that will be used, cherished, and remembered for years. Her daughters spent lots of time with Linda's mom, and they adored her, naming each of their daughters with their grandmother's name as their middle name. Linda is following in her mother's footsteps; her grandchildren are the highlight of her life, and she is theirs. She always does the traditional seven fishes on Christmas Eve with the whole family, ever the good Italian Mama. With a lousy hip, she has sadly declared her retirement from rowing. How will we ever get our gossip?

Ann retired from all the day-to-day mayhem and stress of her job. She, too, has a grandson who is the most handsome baby I have ever seen. He is the Bradley Cooper of babies. I keep trying to talk them into getting him an agent, but they have their hands full with jobs, a new house, and the Cooper look-alike, who is still in diapers. Since her daughter is only a short drive away, Ann frequently drives to New Jersey to give her daughter and son-in-law a bit of a break. I think she relishes taking care of the delightful Marcus.

Not wanting a moment of boredom to settle in after retirement, she promptly got a part-time job volunteering at Longwood Gardens. She meets lots of new folks and has free access to all the lightshows and concerts. She loves it. She continues to row as often as she can.

Lou is still working but vows these are the last few years for her. She used to adore the start-up company and its culture that she worked for, but as with many successful companies, they were purchased by a group who had their own ideas of culture, so things aren't what they used to be for her.

She has her hands full at home with her ninety-four-year-old father (who is still gardening and has a sweetie), her thirty-something daughter who adores her grandad, a working husband, two cats, and two dogs. They have been renovating the wonderful old farmhouse they own for the last several years. At one point, they decided to refinish all the wood floors in the house at once to get the nasty job done and over with. Since it would require moving all furniture out of most rooms and result in dust everywhere for four weeks, she moved the family (including the nonhuman critters) to a B&B on a lake five hours away.

She still skates with Stephanie, Thumper, and Reid and will soon start curling lessons. This may be the new winter sport. Without our Linda powerhouse and no one to count strokes, we will never be the Pink Panthers.

I didn't get to row as much as I wanted last year. It was personally the year from hell. We downsized, sold our house, renovated a retirement cottage, and moved for the first time in thirty-five years. And, as if this wasn't enough distraction, my husband had two hip operations with complications from one resulting in a third operation, and my dog suffered from a broken leg falling out of a car window. I tried to get onto the water a few times, and when I did, it was glorious. I loved being on the water, in that quad or my single, as much as I did the first time I rowed so many years ago.

Here's hoping the coming years will be at least a shred more uneventful and that I will have time to get back to rowing until I drop. I always have my single, and maybe I will find myself in a quad, maybe with Lou and Ann again. Maybe not.

The Panthers filled the role of the family that I never had. They cemented the holes in my life with the unconditional love that comes along for the ride on the shoulders of true friends. They are my sisters.

Acknowledgments

The Wilmington Rowing Center (WRC) is on the picturesque and always-full-of-surprises Christina River in Wilmington, Delaware. The rowing center has existed for over 30 years, supporting a primarily masters and small scholastic rowing programs. Membership fluctuates but is usually around 180 active rowers. Rowing coaches nationwide have praised it as one of the most well-run clubs, a testament to its unique features and engaged members.

We own our building (well, us and the bank) on the river and a substantial fleet of boats, paid for by dues, our annual regatta, and a capital campaign. That regatta is the Diamond States Masters Regatta (DSMR), a favorite of racers who love the venue and the care with which the volunteers (WRC members) organize and run the two days of racing. As many as 1000 rowers from up and down the East Coast travel to compete, bringing their families to enjoy Noxonton Pond. We have been allowed to use this pond for our regatta for over 25 years because one of the founders of DSMR, John Schoonover, is an alumna of Saint Andrews School (the site of the movie "Dead Poets Society)," whose campus includes the pond.

The Wilmington Rowing Center (WRC) has not just been a place for rowing but a community that has welcomed me (and all other newcomers) with open arms. The members of WRC have been the source of many cherished memories and super fun stories. Their camaraderie has been my lifeline and joy; I am deeply grateful to every member who has rowed there.

I'm indebted to Lou, Linda, and Ann for their friendship, laughter, and tolerance of my bowing, which often got us into jams. The Panthers are the core of this story. I am deeply grateful for your presence in my life and the joy you have brought to our rowing experiences.

Thanks to my very good friend Ann Murphy for her first-pass edit, which was a crawl-on-your-knees-over-broken-glass experience, to my sister-in-law, Heidi Bowers, who got me interested in the sport in the first place, and to my husband Paul Halter who during rowing season often had to make appointments to see me since I was out rowing so much.

I also owe Wayne Anthony Conaway of West Chester, PA, a debt of gratitude. Tony encouraged me to continue writing when we were members of the "Pens on Fire" writing group. Tony created the book's name and some of its funnier renditions. Tony passed away in January 2021.

By the way, the WRC women's racing team has not always been and is not currently as described. Best of all, the Christina River has been cleaned up considerably since I began rowing. I doubt if it could be used to remove warts anymore!

In case you have become intrigued, WRC offers learn-to-row programs every May and June. Just saying . . .